The
ELUSIVE
PURPLE
GANG

Detroit's Kosher Nostra

Gregory A. Fournier

Published by Wheatmark®
2030 East Speedway Boulevard, Suite 106
Tucson, Arizona 85719 USA
www.wheatmark.com

ISBN: 978-1-62787-714-5 (paperback)
ISBN: 978-1-62787-715-2 (ebook)
LCCN: 2019912373

Bulk ordering discounts are available through Wheatmark, Inc.
For more information, email orders@wheatmark.com or call
1-888-934-0888.

rev202001
3 9082 14187 9067

Contents

— 1 —

Purple Gang Origins

THE FOLK HISTORY OF Detroit's Purple Gang has acquired a great deal of embroidery not found in the original fabric. Crime magazines, pulp fiction, and movies have helped perpetuate the romanticized image of gangsters as antiheroes fighting a corrupt economic system. The glamor of wealth and power portrayed masks the grim reality of underworld life. History is often rewritten to fit our myths, and so it is with gangsters. With heavily armed thugs committing murder and mayhem on Detroit's streets with impunity during Prohibition, nobody was safe from their brand of urban terrorism.

After the horrors of World War I and mechanized warfare, the generation of young Americans in the 1920s was not interested in the hypocrisy of the past. They were more open-minded than their elders. This new generation quit believing in yesterday's heroes. The horse and buggy age gave way to the automobile, and the birds shared the skies with airplanes. Telephones made communication over long distances instantaneous, and motion pictures brought mass entertainment to national audiences. These mechanical marvels made modern life possible.

This post–World War I generation helped reshape American culture in the 1920s like nothing had before. This new age was ripe with possibilities, and young people were intoxicated by its prospects. In this brave new world, the distinction between good and bad became blurred. It was as easy for a good man to do bad things as it was for a bad man to do good things. In this morally ambivalent postwar world, the Purple Gang loomed large in Detroit.

How the Purple Gang came by their name is a matter of conjecture. Legend has it that an Eastern Market butcher complained to a cop on his beat about the band of delinquent street kids who robbed him blind and vandalized his business. "Those boys are purple like rotten meat," he said. Other people think the gang earned its name during the Cleaners and Dyers War (1925–1928) when they strong-armed the Detroit laundry industry into their racket-run Wholesale Cleaners and Dyers Association. Independent laundry operators who refused to join the gang's association had purple dye thrown onto their customers' clothes. Few small businessmen could sustain that level of liability.

Anybody who got in the gang's way was beaten or killed, with many cleaning plants and laundry shops torched or dynamited. Such strong-arm tactics earned the early gang its reputation for ruthless violence. Independent laundry operators were terrified and quickly driven out of business. Then a gang-approved owner took over the business and began selling booze and running numbers out the back door while they laundered clothes and money through the front door.

Another rumor about the Purple Gang name went that some younger foot soldiers began wearing suits with custom purple linings to play off of the color imagery. Not likely. Yet another story holds that Eddie Fletcher—a Purple Gang gunman from New York—was a featherweight boxer who wore a purple robe and trunks when fighting. Fletcher's ring career was mixed, and soon he became a boxing manager and personal bodyguard for Purple Gang liquor distributor Johnny Reid.

The most documented source for the Purple Gang name comes from a March 19, 1939, article in the *Detroit Times* written by reporter John M. Carlisle. He wrote that Detroit police inspector Henry Joseph Garvin claimed, "I'm the gent who gave the Purps [sic] their moniker. It was in late 1927 when the Cleaners and Dyers War was waging. We got a tip about a mob of young hoodlums who were terrorizing businessmen in the laundry industry. We pinched the whole lot of those young punks at their hangout. They were from seventeen to twenty-four years of age."

The inspector and his crime and bomb squad took the young thugs to police headquarters for their first group roundup photo, where they tried to look tough for each other but held their fedoras hiding their faces. Garvin recognized the group as a band of Jewish street toughs from the Hastings Street area in Paradise Valley who as teens stole from local truck farmers and handcart operators at Detroit's Eastern Market. The youth gang had driven Hastings Street merchants crazy with petty crimes like shoplifting and vandalism. As the boys grew older, they began to roll drunks and rob anyone who looked like they had money in their pockets.

Inspector Garvin was quoted further in the article: "Some newspaper men came to the 13th Precinct Station and started asking questions about the mass arrest. 'I know these punks. They hang around with an Oakland Sugar House gent named Sammy Purple,' I said. 'They're probably Purple's gang.' The reporters liked the label and started using the phrase 'the so-called Purple Gang' in their papers. From then on, these hoods were known as the Purple Gang."

The gang hated the name. Whenever alleged Purple Gang members were arrested or interrogated, they denied there was a Purple Gang. Early gang member Joe "Honey Boy" Miller complained to a reporter that he'd like to find the guy who came up with that name. "The Purple Gang stuff makes me sick. Who thought up that name?"

By the very nature of their illegal businesses, criminals are clandestine figures. The less that is known about their organization and their members, the more likely their enterprises will be successful. The gangsters' basic business model was simple—operate away from the scrutiny of the police and the press. Notoriety and publicity were bad for business. Once the phrase "so-called Purple Gang" started appearing in the newspapers, it seemed like every unsolved crime or murder in Detroit brought suspicion and their name to the front pages.

But by the end of the Roaring Twenties, the Detroit police claimed that the Purple Gang was responsible for five hundred solved and unsolved local murders from 1925 to 1929, without offering any proof to support that large number. Detroit, Hamtramck, Grosse Pointe, and Downriver had no shortage of local gangs who were willing to kill people if they got in their way or double-crossed them. As the Purple Gang tightened its grip on Detroit crime, their high-profile murders appeared regularly in the newspapers. Public outrage against the rampant violence was countered by fear of what would happen if you testified against them.

From 1880 through 1924, four million Jewish people from Russia, Poland, and the Austria-Hungary Empire migrated to America. Many families were drawn to Detroit by the promise of the booming industrial economy. From 1910 to 1920, Detroit's immigrant population doubled, making the city the fourth largest American city—up from number seven. Foreign-born residents accounted for 29 percent of the city's residents. Detroit was the fastest growing and most dynamic urban area in the post–World War I era. The automobile business was burgeoning, and the factories and steel mills were hiring.

The 1920s brought an unprecedented building boom to Detroit's downtown area, defining the city's skyline for the next forty years with buildings like the fifteen-story Maccabees Building; the twenty-nine-story Book-Cadillac Hotel, with its copper-clad roof; the thirty-six-story Guardian Building—nicknamed the "Cathedral of Finance"; and the tallest skyscraper in Detroit—the forty-seven-story Penobscot Building. The city's cultural center boasted an impressive main library, Wayne State University, and the Detroit Institute of Arts. The 1920s also brought the opening of the Ambassador Bridge to Canada and the Detroit-Windsor Vehicular Tunnel in 1930, which became conduits for international commerce and the illegal importation of alcohol from Canada. Detroit was a city on the rise attracting every manner of entrepreneur—including the criminal element. The city was awash with money and ripe for exploitation.

Outside the city's burgeoning downtown business and banking center, Detroit was a low-rise city. Because of vast areas of flat farmland available for building, the city built outward rather than upward as New York City had done. The sprawling auto factories radiated from the downtown area to the outskirts of the city. The auto plants were surrounded by low-income, one- and two-family wood-frame houses spread out for miles in every direction on streets lined with elm or maple trees. In most parts of the city, the highest visible buildings were factory smokestacks and church steeples.

The Jewish community, like previous ethnic immigrants, settled in the poorest inner-city areas. In their ethnic Detroit neighborhood of Paradise Valley, their housing may have been run down and aging, but it was better than the high-rise tenement districts in New York City with little sunshine or open space for children to play.

The original Purple Gang members grew up on Detroit's lower east side in a tenement district city officials and police called "the ghetto"—an unfit slum of aging wooden homes and urban blight. Its residents called their neighborhood "Little Jerusalem." Most of the early gang members were first-generation Americans of Russian and Polish immigrants who left their countries to escape czarist Russian pogroms and the growing tide of European antisemitism. They were hardworking, clannish, and cautious about the foreign world they found themselves in. Most elderly, Jewish adults spoke only Yiddish, further isolating them from mainstream America.

The opportunities most European immigrants sought in their new country were tempered by the harsh reality of living in the worst, most-crowded tenement districts America's large cities had to offer. These congested, bustling neighborhoods developed a Yiddish culture rich with literature, music, and song often dealing with the plight of the immigrant worker struggling to fit into an unwelcoming social and political atmosphere. Jewish entertainers and comedians invented vaudeville, which was a comfort to the Jewish community. These newly arrived European Jews developed solidarity and a shared group consciousness within their tight-knit communities. Many of these people were businessmen in the Old Country. In this New World, Jews saved what they could of their old culture and developed an ethnic market economy of dry-goods stores, bakeries, delicatessens, fish markets, vegetable pushcarts, drug stores, boarding houses, hotels, barber shops, health clinics, and more than their share of saloons, pool halls, and pawn shops.

Unwelcoming Americans eyed the mass migration of Eastern Europeans who spoke different languages, practiced a different religion, and held onto their Old World customs as a threat to the American way of life. Many Eastern European Jews supported socialistic principles as a means of securing economic and social equality. Their shared experiences helped create a strong link between the Jewish community and liberal political movements—which created suspicion among American capitalists and the Protestant ruling elite.

Jewish immigrant parents typically had large families and were hard-pressed to understand or meet the needs of their children in a country they were unfamiliar with. Immigrant children collided head-on with American culture in the public schools—but as the children's English language skills improved—the young children learned how to get along in a culture foreign to them. They helped their parents navigate American society acting as translators, facilitators, or enablers. While the children's world expanded, their parents clung to their Old World traditions and native languages. Their children were restless to rise up from the ghetto and climb the social ladder as seamlessly as possible. For some kids, this meant a life of crime.

Most children of immigrant Americans worked hard to get an education or some on-the-job training to advance their station in life, help their families, and improve their communities. But some kids didn't take well to public school. They got their education on the streets where they spent much of their time. Inner-city schools generally lacked a gym, a playground, or a sports field, and afterschool programs were nonexistent. Classroom discipline was harsh, and difficult students were labeled as "problem children."

The original Purple Gang members were segregated on the upper floor of the Old Bishop School, which was dedicated to training delinquent students for the manual trades, preparing them for a life toiling in Detroit's sweat shop factories. These kids saw their parents and neighbors coming home weary and worn after a long day of hard work and low pay. Working as a human cog in the machinery of an automobile plant held no charm or promise for these restless teens.

The Old Bishop School is where the Burnstein brothers, the Keywell brothers, and the Fleisher brothers met other rebellious kids from the neighborhood and formed a street gang that created its own culture, operated by its own rules, and meted out its own rough code of justice. Many of these boys became newsboys and learned the ways of the street at an early age. Newspapers were bought two for a nickel from newspaper distributors and then sold for a nickel apiece, doubling the boys' money.

A busy street corner was a prized location that had to be defended to discourage competitors, so the boys banded together with their friends to stake their street corner claims. These kids grew up tough. Joseph and Raymond Burnstein discovered the value of threats and violence in establishing a pecking order dominating other newsboys. They had a territory to defend. When they walked the streets of their neighborhood, other kids stepped aside. These boys enjoyed pitching pennies, shooting craps, harassing merchants, smoking cigarettes, and fighting rival youth gangs. The older they became, the more serious their crimes became.

There was another manner of man on Hastings Street that attracted the attention of these untethered street toughs—local underworld figures who didn't work regular jobs or come home grimy and exhausted after a day of hard labor in a factory. These self-made men wore nice clothes and polished shoes as they strolled through the neighborhood greeting and shaking the hands of merchants as they passed their storefronts. These guys seemed to know everyone. They drove flashy cars and hung out in pool rooms and beer gardens most of the day. These men knew how to play the system. The impressionable boys learned street math early—two plus two is four, but five will get you ten if you learn how to work it.

The Russian-born Burnstein parents warned their children to stay away from "trombeniks" (no-good bums), but the boys wanted to be "shtarkers" (tough guys). It wasn't long before the nascent Purples attracted the notice of established neighborhood mobsters in the Oakland Sugarhouse Gang. It was a short step from random juvenile delinquency to professional criminality. Soon, Joe and Ray

Burnstein and their neighborhood street gang graduated
from petty crime and hooliganism to armed robbery, hijacking, extortion, bombing, kidnapping, and murder.

By the early 1920s, the young thugs were mentored by
the leaders of the Sugar House operation, led by Charles
Leiter and Henry Shorr. They were owners of a legitimate
business that sold corn sugar and other home-brewing
supplies like yeast and wort. But the business was actually
a front to launder money from their illegal hijacking, extortion, and distillery business. The Sugar House Gang set up
the equipment in unused warehouses and vacant barns in
the countryside and supplied the raw ingredients for large-
scale brewing plants and distilleries.

Sugar House member Sam "Sammy Purple" Cohen
taught the young thugs the finer points of hijacking, col-
lecting protection money from speakeasies, and extorting
money from legitimate local businessmen, often assaulting
them in the process. If those tactics were ineffective, businesses might be stench bombed or dynamited. The former
street gang terrorized and exploited businesses in their own
neighborhood earning them a reputation for unmitigated
violence. Before long, the Purple Gang's high-profile tactics
drew the attention of Inspector Henry J. Garvin of the crime
and bomb squad.

The Purple Gang was never a well-organized group.
They were a loosely controlled confederation of young thugs
with no recognized leader or mob boss. But Joe and Ray
Burnstein managed the overall operation of the gang with
the help of their oldest and youngest brothers, Abe and Izzy,
who worked in the background. Unlike Italian gangs with
a capo regime and a rigid chain of command, the Purples
allowed their members to branch out and work with non-

Jewish gangsters to pursue what they held in common—the accumulation of ill-gotten goods and easy money. The amount of ethnic cooperation among Detroit's gangs in the early years of Prohibition benefited everyone.

As the Purple Gang prospered and expanded its operations, they took their money and opened speakeasies, nightclubs, and gambling spots. As their territory and interests grew, the Purples began to import members from New York and St. Louis when they needed out-of-town muscle. New York City gangland enforcers like Eddie Fletcher, Abe Axler, and Irving Milberg answered the call. Several former members of Egan's Rats from St. Louis also found work with the Purple Gang on Detroit's mean streets—people like Johnny Reid, Ezra Milford Jones, Gus Winkler, and Fred "Killer" Burke. The rest of Detroit's underworld took notice.

Once the gang was firmly established in the illegal liquor industry, the Purples employed hundreds of people to run their bootlegging, speakeasy, and gambling operations providing refreshment and entertainment to thousands of thirsty Detroiters. The Purple Gang's cottage industry of hijacking liquor shipments, cutting the booze, and relabeling it for retail sale, soon grew to become interstate commerce. The Purple Gang supplied Canadian liquor to Al Capone's organization in Chicago to the west and Frankie Yale in New York City to the east.

Throughout the 1920s, the press reinforced the perception that the Purples were prosecution proof. Many known Purple Gang members developed long rap sheets, but the authorities were never able to make the charges stick. A combination of slick lawyers, shrewd payoffs to influential people, and an absence of witnesses willing to testify gave the gang the illusion of immunity from prosecution.

These Jewish hoodlums instilled fear in their community by the level of violence they were prepared to unleash on anybody opposing them. Citizens victimized by the Purples were deathly afraid to testify. Witnesses routinely left town or simply vanished. Sometimes, the bodies of competitors, double-crossers, or stool pigeons were found bleeding on Detroit's streets or floating face down in the Detroit River on their way to Lake Erie. Witnesses were not lining up to testify against the Purple Gang, and other Detroit gangs were not anxious to battle with them either.

Anyone who double-crossed the gang wasn't safe—even police. Generally, it was wiser for a gang to pay off the local cops to turn a blind eye to speakeasies rather than kill them. But on the afternoon of January 30, 1928, Patrolman Vivian Welch was gunned down for extorting money from Purple Gang's speakeasies beyond his routine payoff. When Welch threatened to rat the gang out if they didn't pay him more hush money, the avaricious twenty-seven-year-old officer sealed his fate. While off duty and dressed in regular street clothes, Welch climbed into a Chevrolet roadster to negotiate his payoff.

When it became apparent Welch was being taken for a ride, he jumped out of the moving car at St. Aubin Street and Faber Avenue in Hamtramck and ran in the opposite direction. The driver slammed on the brakes, and two men jumped out of the back seat, chasing Welch while firing their pistols. One of the shots hit Welch in the back and brought him down. The two men ran up to the wounded police officer and shot him eight more times, execution-style in the head. Both assassins returned to the Chevy, and the wheelman ran over Welch's body as they fled the scene.

A woman from the neighborhood witnessed the shooting

and wrote down the license plate number of the getaway car. The police were able to trace the car to Raymond Burnstein, who was immediately picked up for questioning. He admitted being a bootlegger and claimed his car was stolen on January 21 by hijackers who took his car and twelve cases of whiskey he was carrying. Burnstein's car was still missing.

When a policeman is slain, his brothers in blue typically go after the cop-killers with uncommon vengeance. In all, over forty murder suspects were rounded up and harassed, but all were released for lack of evidence. Eight days after the very public shooting, Police Superintendent James Sprott went before the press with what police were able to discover about Vivian Welch's murder.

"Officer Vivian Welch was shaking down speakeasy owners, violating his oath to uphold the law He was lining his pockets dishonestly. I don't want to be cold-blooded, but I will say he got what was coming to him. Any policeman who does what Welch did will get what's coming to him, just as Welch did."

Nobody ever went to trial for Welch's killing. The murder cemented the reputation of the Purple Gang as a ruthless and unforgiving outfit. As the Oakland Sugarhouse Gang was shut down permanently with many of its key members serving long prison terms for running large-scale distilleries in 1928, other members not imprisoned segued into the Purple Gang's growing orbit. Where one gang ended and the other began is difficult to chart, as many members belonged to both organizations.

The 1930 Chicago Crime Commission—a nonpartisan civic watchdog organization—in its study of Chicago crime found an unholy alliance between crime and politics.

"Politics is a feudal relationship," the report stated, "based not on the law but upon personal loyalties. This is why politicians and criminal gangs understand one another so well and frequently enter into alliances with each other against the more remote common good."

The politics of "who you know and what-have-you-done-for-me-lately" are more important to decision making than the relative merits of any particular issue. The short-term necessity of politicians to get reelected and the gangsters' ability to deliver large blocks of voters contributes to the murky relationship between gangsters and politicians.

During the Prohibition years, the Purple Gang developed into one of the most successful and wealthy criminal enterprises in the nation and the only Jewish crime organization to control the rackets of an entire large American city. Their power reached into city hall, police headquarters, and the Wayne County criminal justice system. If any criminals wanted to operate in Detroit, they needed the approval of the Purple Gang, pay them a percentage of their action, or take their business elsewhere. Otherwise, the consequences would be catastrophic.

—2—

Prohibition Becomes Law

THE MICHIGAN LEGISLATURE PASSED the Damon Act on May 1, 1917, making Michigan a dry state three years before national Prohibition. The manufacture, sale, and distribution of alcohol for private consumption were outlawed. The Detroit underworld had a head start establishing smuggling networks and making business connections with Canadian distillers before national Prohibition took effect in the rest of the nation in 1920.

Despite a veto by President Woodrow Wilson, two-thirds of the state legislators voted to make the Eighteenth Amendment to the Constitution and the Volstead Act the law of the land. National Prohibition set into motion more carnage for the people of the United States than any legislative act since the Civil War. The act sought to ensure that "no person shall manufacture, sell, barter, transport, import, export, deliver, or furnish intoxicating liquors except as authorized by this act." The provisions, fines, and penalties were spelled out in great detail, but the act failed to specifically prohibit the purchase or consumption of intoxicating liquors creating a law enforcement nightmare. Social commentator and news-paper columnist Will Rogers quipped that Prohibition was "better than no liquor at all." Rogers's observation characterized the attitude of many Americans during the Roaring Twenties.

National Prohibition took effect on January 16, 1920. At first, Michiganders simply drove across the Ohio state line to purchase their alcohol beverages, but soon the Michigan State Police began enforcing the law and laid in wait to arrest offenders as they crossed the state line. The city of Detroit was strategically located only a watery mile from the distilleries and breweries of its Canadian neighbor Windsor, Ontario.

River smuggling was a free-for-all in the beginning. Anyone with a boat could get in on the action, but it wasn't long before organized gangs began staking out territory. Independent operators were either forced out of business or they began working for the underworld as associates. More often than not, the early Purple Gang hijacked shipments of illegal booze from other gangs and independent bootleggers, leaving many truck drivers traumatized or dead. The Purple Gang started out as small-time hoods and thieves but grew to manhood with the emergence of Prohibition making them rich men in short order.

By 1929, the bootlegging business was Detroit's second-leading industry behind the automobile business. Auto factories provided the underworld with thousands of thirsty customers who regarded Prohibition as a bad law to openly violate. The three Bs—"booze, betting, and broads"—sent many a factory worker home with little or no money from their hard-earned paycheck.

Protestant ministers—Methodists in particular—craved

a stricter moral climate because they believed that demon rum was responsible for public drunkenness, domestic violence, child abuse, idiocy, and moral turpitude. Henry Ford attributed alcohol as the major cause for the 25 percent absentee rate of his daily workforce. Ford—a stern Episcopalian Protestant—was a major funder of the Temperance Movement. If his workers came to work smelling of liquor, they were summarily fired.

Many factors lead to national Prohibition despite the unpopularity of the law with a large portion of the public. During World War I, the federal government of the United States diverted grain products to the war effort, cutting off supplies for brewers and distillers setting the stage for Prohibition after the war ended in 1919. In that same year, American women won the right to vote when the Nineteenth Amendment was ratified giving them real political clout for the first time.

Alcoholism was destructive to family life and a big problem in America. Many drunken husbands gambled away their paychecks, missed work, beat their wives, abused or neglected their children, and deserted their families. Women like Susan B. Anthony and Elizabeth Cady Stanton rebelled against the abuse of women at the hands of drunken men and led the anti-saloon movement. Fifty years of temperance campaigns kept the issue before the American public, and the alliance of puritanical politicians with women's temperance groups proved a powerful political alliance. Angry evangelists like Sister Amy Semple, Brother Billy Sunday, and Reverend J. O. L. Sprecklin in Ontario railed against the evils of demon rum.

Another underlying cause of Prohibition was rural America's paranoia about the growing urban influence of big cities in American life. The turn of the twentieth century shifted America's demographic from a rural farm economy to an urban industrial economy. Once American farm boys went to "Gay Paree" during World War I, it was hard to keep them tied to the plow. Residents of the heartland developed anti-immigrant feelings against northern and eastern European immigrants crowding into America's urban areas. They feared the large influx of European Catholic and Jewish immigrants whose customs they feared would impact negatively on American culture and their way of life.

Despite the sincere belief that making alcohol illegal would cure many of America's social ills, Prohibition was the catalyst for rum-running, bootlegging, organized crime, and their attendant vices—gambling, prostitution, and murder. The Detroit Police estimated over five hundred mob-related murders occurred between 1920 and 1929— many attributed rightly or wrongly to the Purple Gang. In 1925 alone, Detroit recorded 232 homicides. Only ten were confirmed gangland murders, seven were slain policemen, and fifty-three were bodies fished out of the Detroit River.

———

Prior to the opening of the International Ambassador Bridge on Friday, November 15, 1929, and the Detroit-Windsor Vehicular Tunnel a year later on November 3, 1930, many Detroiters relied on the Walkerville & Detroit Ferry Service to transport themselves across the Detroit River to Windsor, Ontario. Every manner of small-scale smuggling was devised by otherwise law-abiding Americans to circumvent the unpopular Prohibition law. Bottle harnesses were worn under clothes, pockets were sewn into overcoats, and secret car compartments were made to bring in the illegal elixir. The international border was porous.

Early in Prohibition, Detroiters canoed, rowed, or sailed across the river, loaded their boats with booze, and returned without any significant resistance—sometimes making the round trip several times a day. During the winter months, large sleds powered by half a dozen harnessed men were sometimes used. Old Model T Fords costing between five and ten dollars were used to cross frozen Lake St. Clair and Lake Erie to keep supply lines open. The doors and roofs were removed from the jalopies to make the loading and unloading of the booze faster and to give the driver a fighting chance to leap from the vehicle if the ice broke. When a jalopy fell through the ice, the smugglers weren't out much except the cost of the booze they couldn't save before the junker sunk. Over the thirteen years of Prohibition, the bottom of Lake St. Clair and Lake Erie were littered with many old cars and cases of Canadian beer and liquor.

The Canadian cities of Windsor, LaSalle, Sandwich, Walkerville, and Ford City were collectively known as the Border Cities. The cities were linked by a system of road-houses and export docks along the shoreline, tempting thirsty Americans with full-strength liquor, beer, and inexpensive all-you-can-eat fried chicken, perch, walleye, and frog-leg dinners. Some places offered free lunches to attract business. Every night, but especially on the weekends, these roadhouse diners provided entertainment with gambling and brothel services quietly quartered on the guarded second floor of their establishments. Americans tying up their boats at roadhouse docks for a night of carousing would often return with as much liquor as their boats could carry.

It wasn't long before Purple Gang associates began hijacking liquor shipments and shooting uncoopera-tive smugglers driving most amateurs out of the business. Soon, several of the larger established gangs carved out territories setting up what amounted to water-taxi services making smuggling liquor a profitable criminal enterprise. The Purple Gang, run by the Burnstein brothers, controlled the Detroit River waterfront. The Italian Eastside Mob of Joe "Uno" Zerilli and William "Black Bill" Tocco claimed the St. Clair River and Lake St. Clair. The Italian West-Side Mob of Cesare "Big Chet" La Mare and Joe Tocco (unre-lated to William) claimed the Rouge River south to Lake Erie. Each of the major players had plenty of territory to work within, and each established their own distribution network of speakeasies and blind pigs.

Speakeasies attracted a more affluent clientele than blind pigs which catered to blue-collar working men and sold whiskey by the shot or beer by the glass. Blind pigs could be found in apartments, basements, garages, or the back rooms of legitimate businesses. Speakeasies developed into nightclubs offering entertainment which introduced white audiences to African American blues and jazz per-formers ushering in a new age of American music. During Prohibition, women were allowed in speakeasies for the first time, creating the "flapper" phenomenon and leading to the popular Charleston dance craze and less restrictive clothing. Young women began to smoke in public, and hip flasks were all the rage.

The Purple Gang was on working terms with their Mafia counterparts. Ethnic cooperation was a factor in the gangs' mutual success. The Purples worked with anyone who could help them achieve their primary objective—making large sums of easy money. Early on, the Purple Gang was better known for hijacking rather than smuggling. Stealing from other renegade crews and independent operators was more profitable and less risky than actual bootlegging. When Chicago's Al Capone wanted to set up operations on the Detroit River, he entered into a lucrative business arrangement, making the Purples his exclusive suppliers of Canadian whiskey catapulting them to the top of Detroit's underworld. Once word of the alliance hit the streets, the Purple Gang gained instant credibility.

As the gang's distribution network grew, they needed a steady supply of product. The Purples enlisted freelance operators to smuggle liquor and beer on their territory if they paid a set amount per case or turned over a percentage of their shipment to the gang. Any resistance met with fatal consequences. As Prohibition dragged on, the Purples gave franchise rights to an affiliated gang called the Third Street Terrors renamed The Little Jewish Navy by the Detroit police. After the gang acquired a fleet of speedboats, they plied the swift-moving current transporting Canadian Whiskey across the river. Government sources estimated that 75 percent of all alcohol smuggled into the United States during Prohibition crossed the Detroit River, earning the Detroit River the nickname "The Detroit-Windsor Funnel."

———

In the spring of 1927, Al "Scarface" Capone was expanding his crime empire by supplying liquor through his growing Midwestern distribution network. There was more demand for Capone liquor than his organization could

supply. Capone cast his eyes east. Only a mile of swift-flow-
ing water separated Detroit from the distilleries and breweries of Canada.

A secret meeting was held at the Fort Shelby Hotel in
Detroit between Capone and the leadership of the Purple
Gang to discuss a business proposition. In a well-protected,
private dining room, the Purples were represented by the
elder statesman of the gang, Abe Burnstein. At thirty-six
years old, Abe was nine years older than his brother Joe,
who was the dapper front man for the gang. His strength
was business management. He operated several businesses
as fronts for money-laundering operations. Ray Burnstein
was one year younger than Joe and the face of the gang on
the street. Ray controlled the muscle. If he came looking for
you, you didn't want to be found. The youngest Burnstein
brother was Isadore. Izzy worked mostly behind the scenes
quietly managing the family's gambling interests. He was
content to let his older brothers run the day-to-day business
of the gang.

The Purple Gang already shared the waterfront with the
Italian Eastside mob from the St. Clair River north and the
Sicilian Westside mob that ruled the Detroit River from the
headwaters of the Rouge River to where the Detroit River
emptied into Lake Erie. The smuggling triad cooperated tol-
erably well as long as the Purple Gang acted as a buffer
between the rival Sicilian and Italian Mafia factions. One
faction was old-school Sicilians, who clung to the old ways.
The other faction was wanted to modernize their operations
and work across ethnic lines with Jewish, Irish, and Polish
gangs. The Italian river gangs were on a collision course.

Control of Detroit's twenty-eight-mile shoreline was
hard won with blood, and the Purple Gang jealously

guarded their smuggling operations on their territory. It was Abe who developed large-scale business ties with Canadian distilleries—principally Hiram Walker. For many years, Abe built political relationships and paid off key Detroit police and border authorities to insure their operation ran as interruption free as possible. Abe paid out the graft. The Purples were not about to let Capone set up a franchise on their territory. The balance of power on the river was fragile, and there was no room for Capone.

The Chicago crime lord brought his business manager Jake "Greasy Thumb" Guzik and his trusted personal bodyguard Jack McGurn to the meeting. Both gangs had their own security strategically positioned in and around the hotel. Capone was on a charm offensive. He explained he was building a Midwestern syndicate that could easily move over one thousand cases of bonded Canadian liquor a week. Capone pointed out how Chicago was ideally situated because of their network hub of five railroad lines and a highway system that branched out into America's heartland. What he needed was a reliable source for Canadian liquor—all the Purples could supply. Capone was willing to pay top dollar for it.

Legend has it that Ray Burnstein told Capone that the Purples controlled all the liquor traffic on the Detroit River and everything that came across, they got a piece of. The Purples weren't interested in giving away any of their waterfront to an out-of-town outfit. Capone wasn't interested in fighting a turf war with the Detroit underworld. Staying out of the cemetery in Chicago was a full-time job for Capone since he took over the Chicago organization from Johnny Torrio in 1922.

Capone and the Purples cut a compromise deal making

the Purple Gang Capone's exclusive suppliers of uncut bonded Canadian whiskey—including his favorite brand, Old Log Cabin bourbon, imported from Montreal, Canada. The Purples earmarked as much bonded Canadian liquor as possible for Capone and safeguarded its passage to St. Joseph, Michigan. Capone's men would take it from there into Chicago. There was plenty of money to be made for everyone Capone assured them as they shook hands sealing the deal. Jake Guzik handed a briefcase packed full of startup money to the Burnsteins said to be $30,000.

Capone's public persona with the Chicago press made him a larger-than-life celebrity gangster. Capone became the most visible and famous underworld figure in the nation. He reveled in his notoriety. Everything he said or did was amplified by the Chicago press and the national newspapers. When word circulated on Detroit streets that the Purple Gang was in league with the Capone organization, the Purple's credibility in the underworld was elevated. No outfit in Detroit dared challenge them. The Capone and Purple Gang business partnership worked well for several years until the federal government began investing large sums of money in coast guard patrol boats and more Prohibition agents.

The Little Jewish Navy faction of the Purple Gang ran a water taxi service smuggling Canadian liquor into Michigan, but with new president Herbert Hoover making a dedicated effort to wipe out bootlegging during his administration, the balance of power on the Detroit River began to change. The riskier the return trip from Canada, the more expensive it was to do business.

Early on, federal law enforcement was not equipped with enough patrol boats or personnel to stem the flow of illegal liquor from Canada. Smugglers operated largely unimpeded. But in the spring of 1928, more federal Prohibition agents and coast guard personnel were hired and equipped with powerful patrol boats armed with machine guns mounted on their bows. Speedboat technology improved, but bootleggers had more disposable income and commissioned sleeker and faster boats. Smugglers devised evasive strategies to avoid capture, but the tide was beginning to turn against them.

When river trafficking became too risky to conduct business, there were other ways of getting liquor across the international border. Massive quantities of illegal liquor entered Detroit via the Michigan Central Train Tunnel under the river. Then, it was shipped nationwide. Because of the high volume of commercial traffic through the international tunnel, police rarely tampered with railroad commerce. Prohibition agents had their hands full patrolling the river and looking for stills and breweries in the city.

The Detroit River could easily be breeched from the sky also. Al Capone bought a fleet of World War I army surplus Curtiss JN-4D bombers. Capone hired former World War I pilots from Selfridge Aero Squadron Base to fly daily shipments from Canada. Each plane held twenty-five cases—three hundred bottles—in its bomb bay. The bomb bay was loaded in under ten minutes, and the pilot would hand a bundle of money wrapped in butcher paper to Blaise Diesbourg, who preferred to be known in the liquor business as King Canada. The planes flew over the Detroit River and landed at secret fields in Michigan.

Diesbourg cut the deal personally with Capone in the

basement of Diesbourg's brother in Belle River, Ontario. King Canada acted as Capone's sole airborne exporter. Diesbourg placed orders at the Canadian export dock and filled out the official Canadian B-13 export papers. King Canada paid cash for the shipment and had it delivered to one of five farm fields he leased in the country. When the planes landed, Diesbourg was a one-man operation loading the twenty-five cases into each plane himself making him a very rich man. These flights continued until the repeal of Prohibition in 1933.

—3—

The Cleaners and Dyers War

1925–1928

THE PURPLE GANG FIRST came to public notice in Detroit when they were linked to what became known as the Cleaners and Dyers War. Early in 1924, a price war raged in the laundry industry driving cleaning and pressing prices down to where the large wholesale cleaning plants were losing money. By 1925, there was a power play for control of the industry.

Legitimate businessman Charles Jacoby Jr., owner of French Dyers and Cleaners; Detroit Federation of Labor president, Frances X. Martel; and silent partner, Abe Burnstein—Jacoby's brother-in-law—entered into a collusive agreement to regulate and control prices in the cleaning industry. Together, they formed the Wholesale Cleaners and Dyers Association, installing Charles Jacoby as the association's first president. Jacoby set union dues at twenty-five dollars a week, but dues were soon raised to 2 percent of each cleaning plant's gross pretax profits putting the squeeze on business owners.

Once the labor racket was operational, Jacoby, Martel, and Burnstein skimmed dues money off the top. A portion of the money was also siphoned off to finance terrorism against operators who refused to cooperate and join their association. When it came to the strong-arm work, the union's board of directors hired younger men to handle the rough stuff.

Abe Burnstein enlisted the aid of his younger brothers Joe and Ray and their street-tough friends to act as recruiters and enforcers persuading stubborn laundry operators to join their union. If friendly persuasion and threats failed, beatings, burnings, and bombings became compelling recruitment methods. The Purple Gang's strong-arm tactics went largely unchallenged for a year, creating fear among legitimate businessmen struggling to scratch out a living in the labor-intensive laundry industry. Some independent operators simply went out of business, others were roughed up, and some mysteriously left town or otherwise disappeared.

When a group of tailors worked up the courage to complain about the exorbitant dues at a Detroit Federation of Labor meeting, President Martel slammed a brick down on the table and warned, "Shut up and sit down if you know what's good for you." Outside the industry, nobody suspected that organized criminals had infiltrated their business organization.

Then on December 9, 1926, the body of Samuel Sigman was found with three gunshot wounds, a broken neck, and crushed ribs on his left side. Police theorized Sigman was shot by an unknown gunman while riding in a car before his body was dumped on the snowy street. Police ruled out robbery as a motive. Sigman's wallet contained money and his Masonic signet ring set with diamonds was still on his right hand. Further police investigation revealed that Sigman was the secretary of the Perfect Dyers and Cleaners Association. With no other leads or witnesses, no connection to the Wholesale Cleaners was established. The case ended up in the cold case file.

Then, early in 1928, the body of Samuel Polakoff—vice president of the Union Cleaners and Dyers Company—was found in the back seat of his parked car, beaten to death with a hammer. The sheer brutality of Polakoff's murder finally broke the code of silence that was the cornerstone of the Purple Gang's power. Despite fearing for their lives, ten cleaning plant operators began explaining to police detectives the reign of terror their industry had worked under for the last three years.

After a business dispute with Jacoby and Burnstein, Martel distanced himself from the Wholesale Cleaners and Dyers Association and eventually turned against them. Then he persuaded several cleaning plant operators to press charges against Jacoby and Burnstein and their Purple Gang thugs. Thirteen alleged Purple Gang members were arrested where the gang hung out in the back of Jacoby's French Dyers and Cleaners business. Joe Burnstein, Ray Burnstein, Harry Fleisher, Ed Fletcher, Irving Shapiro, Harry Keywell, Phil Keywell, Irving Milberg, Joe Miller, Abe Miller, Abe Axler, Sam Axler, and George Cordell were rounded up by Inspector Harry Garvin and his men from the crime and bomb squad. The group was photographed, fingerprinted, and held on extortion charges.

Two people named in the indictment were arrested elsewhere. Oakland Sugar House business manager John (Jack) Wolff was picked up at the Oakland Sugar House and Abe

Burnstein was out of town attending an Atlantic City crime conference with the likes of New York boyhood friends Meyer Lansky and Charles "Lucky" Luciano. His business associate Al Capone was also in attendance. When Abe returned to Detroit from the conference, he surrendered to authorities with his lawyer Edward Kennedy Jr., who posted $500 bail for Abe's release.

Comparative calm settled over Detroit while the Cleaners and Dyers defendants awaited trial. On the street, the case became known as the Purple Gang Case. For a month, police received no reports of stench bombings, theft or vandalism of cleaning company delivery trucks, beatings, bombings, or shootings. The calm was attributed to the curtailment of the Purple Gang's movements.

At the trial, defense attorney Samuel J. Rhodes asked why Francis Martel was not called as a witness. "It clearly appears that Martel is inextricably linked with, participated in, and is connected with the entire series of events which the allegations against my clients are based. Any conspiracy to extort money clearly benefited Martel, who conspired to put Charles Jacoby out of business and instigated the charge against him. Martel has manipulated the cleaning and dyers business as a means to control the labor unions."

Judge Charles Bowles of Recorder's Court agreed to issue a bench warrant for Martel to testify, but the Detroit Federation of Labor leader couldn't be found. The prosecutor informed Judge Bowles that Martel was on union business outside the jurisdiction of the court giving no further details.

In his opening remarks to the jury, Defense Attorney Rhodes stated that Francis Martel and his partner Henry Rosman—proprietor of the Famous Cleaners and Dyers—

were chiefly responsible for the fraud, violence, and terrorism of the Cleaners and Dyers War. "The 'Purple Gang' was a fiction created by Rosman." Rhodes explained to the court that Abe Burnstein was taken into the organization to act as a peacemaker and arbitrator who reluctantly accepted the job. Rhodes accused Francis Martel of double-crossing workers organized in his union for his own profit. When his union members demanded shorter hours and overtime pay, Martel refused to negotiate for them and was paid $700 by the Wholesale and Dyers Association as a payoff.

On the stand, Henry Rosman testified that Abe Burnstein told him he was a fool for paying $144 a day for twelve security guards to protect his drivers. Burnstein explained that he was in a position to make peace in the industry if Rosman would pay the Wholesale Cleaners and Dyers Association $100 a week. That would save him over $1,900 a month and end his labor troubles. Rosman testified he told Burnstein, "You and your men are the reason I hired security guards. Your own brother Ray is involved."

Burnstein denied it.

"Objection!" Defense Attorney Rhoades said. "I move to have that last remark about my client's brother stricken from the record. It assumes facts not in evidence."

"Sustained, Mr. Rhoades."

What Wayne County prosecutors believed to be an open-and-closed case of extortion was compromised by Martel's absence and the recanting of the extortion complaint against Jacoby—and the others—by two laundry and dry-cleaning plant operators William B. Manisajian and Willard J. Webster. They denied on the witness stand their earlier statements to police investigators. Other potential witnesses could not be found to testify. The focus of the case shifted to the labor dispute rather than the conspiracy to extort money.

On September 13, 1928, the cleaners and dyers case was given to the jury. After a hotly contested three-week trial, the jury returned a not-guilty verdict acquitting all defendants in under an hour of deliberation. The only results of the case were the Cleaners and Dyers War ended and the Purple Gang's reputation for immunity from prosecution was born. Extensive daily newspaper coverage put the Purple Gang name before the Detroit public for months giving the gang marquee status.

—4—

Milaflores Apartment Massacre

JOHNNY REID WAS A former Egan's Rats gangster out of St. Louis, Missouri. Egan's Rats specialized in bank robberies and armored car heists. They were also bootleggers, kidnappers, and contract killers. Reid relocated to Detroit in 1924, where he opened a speakeasy after nine of the Rats' key members were convicted and sentenced to twenty-five years in federal prison for a United States Mail payroll robbery in Staunton, Illinois.

When Johnny Reid arrived to make his fortune in Detroit's bootlegging industry, he hired a young, former prizefighter named Eddie Fletcher as his personal bodyguard. Fletcher was an up-and-coming Purple Gang enforcer imported from New York City. Their personal friendship led to a business partnership with the Purples when Reid became a Midwest distributor for Purple Gang liquor, much of it cut-rate rotgut, but people in the heartland were glad to get it.

Johnny Reid is often credited with pioneering the mob's snatch racket in Detroit. Kidnapping and ransoming wealthy gamblers and racketeers proved to be a profitable sideline in the 1920s when many Detroiters were doing well in the boom times of the auto industry. Once a potential victim was identified as wealthy, he was tailed and his movements and habits were noted. The surprised person was quietly and quickly apprehended, bound, and blindfolded before being driven to one of several safe houses scattered around town. Hostages were terrorized if uncooperative and forced to call their wives or business associates to cough up some money or else. Reid calculated correctly that underworld characters and wealthy gamblers would rather pay the ransom than draw unwanted attention to their activities. The snatch racket was attractive because if planned and executed carefully, it was much safer than other mob rackets.

Ransoms ranged from $10,000 to $25,000 depending on how well-heeled the hostage was. Payoff instructions included where to take the money if they ever wanted to see the hostage alive again. Most importantly, do not contact the police. After the families or associates were squeezed hard, the gang would usually settle for a smaller amount. Murder only complicated matters.

A wave of kidnappings swept the Detroit area in the 1920s prompting industrialist Henry Ford to hire former navy boxer and all-round tough guy Harry Bennett as his personal bodyguard. Despite no previous experience or training in industrial security, Bennett soon became the head of Ford Motor Company's infamous Security Department, known primarily for trying to bust the United Auto Workers union. Henry Ford greatly feared he or a family member would be kidnapped.

As the primarily Jewish Purple Gang gained prominence in the Detroit underworld for ruthless violence, so did Ford's right-hand man—Harry Bennett. Rather than use the Purple Gang for his anti-labor muscle, Bennett hired Mafia muscle. Henry Ford was a known anti-Semite who bought the failing Dearborn Publishing Company in 1919 and began publishing *The Dearborn Independent*, known for its unprecedented attacks on Jews. Issues of the newspaper were widely circulated, and a copy was placed in every new Ford sold. It should be noted that no kidnappers in the Detroit area dared arouse the ire of the bow-tie-wearing Bennett and his no-nonsense Ford security department which had the might of the Dearborn police behind them. No kidnapping attempts were made on the well-protected Ford family.

———

A transplanted Chicago hood by the name of Mike Dipisa came to Detroit and tried to extort money from Johnny Reid's speakeasy. Dipisa sent two thugs to Reid's establishment to threaten and extort money from him. Reid and his bodyguard/bouncer Eddie Fletcher beat up the men and threw them into the street. Furious, Reid placed a call to his former Egan's Rats friend, gunman Fred "Killer" Burke. Burke answered the call and drove immediately up to Detroit.

Burke teamed up with known Purple Gang gunmen Abe Axler and Eddie Fletcher and cruised Detroit's mean streets in a touring car searching for Dipisa at his favorite night haunts. When Dipisa's flashy roadster was spotted, the touring car pulled alongside and opened fire. A gun battle raged while the cars sped down the street side by side. Two policemen walking their beat witnessed men shooting at each other as their cars sped past. The police commandeered a taxi cab and raced after the gangsters' cars. The touring car forced the smaller roadster to the curb with the police in hot pursuit before fleeing the scene. The police pulled up and arrested the three men in the roadster. They denied firing any guns, and no weapons were found on them or in their car.

A second attempt on Dipisa's life occurred a few days later shaking the already shaken Chicago hood. Dipisa asked Johnny Reid for a truce and sued for peace. He told Reid there had been a misunderstanding. The thugs who tried to threaten him were not his men. They were independent contractors who dropped his name to shift the blame on him. The next day, two men were found in a vacant, weed-covered city lot shot to death.

Reid felt satisfied that his street reputation was restored. He continued his liquor distribution business as usual until one early December morning in 1926 when Reid pulled his car into his apartment's parking lot. A single gunman stepped out of the shadows with a sawed-off shotgun and splattered Reid's brain across the inside of his windshield. This affront to the Purple Gang's power would not go answered. The Purples were moved to avenge the death of their business associate and friend.

Rumor on the street pointed the finger at Chicago gunman Frankie "the Pollack" Wright as the killer who was hired by Mike Dipisa to snuff out Johnny Reid. Despite their involvement in the Cleaners and Dyers War at the time, the Purples hatched a plan to lure Wright to his death. Wright was a renegade hood from Chicago, operating several independent gambling joints skirting Purple Gang territory.

Not only did the Purples want to avenge Reid's murder, they also wanted to send a lethal message to anyone who dared muscle in on the Purple Gang's territory, the heart of which ran between Clairmount and Pingree streets west from Woodward Avenue to Grand River Avenue. When Purple Gang drug peddler Jake Weinberg was gunned down on February 3, 1927, by Frank Wright and two cohorts in Purple Gang territory, the Burnsteins vowed revenge.

Rival casino operator Meyer "Fish" Bloomfield—aligned with Mike Dipisa's growing gambling outfit—was kidnapped and held for ransom by the Purple Gang toward the end of March. After Bloomfield was out of circulation for a few days, Frankie Wright received a phone call demanding $40,000 for Bloomfield's ransom. When the ransom was paid, Wright would get another call and be told where and when to pick up the hostage. The trap was set.

Apartment 308 at the fashionable Miraflores Apartments at 106 Alexandrine Drive was the safe house where Bloomfield was held. Frankie "the Pollack" Wright, George "Rube" Cohen, and Joe Bloom arrived at the apartment building at 4:20 a.m. to retrieve Bloomfield. The three men walked cautiously to the stairwell and climbed quietly to the third floor. They peered down the empty hallway before walking to apartment 308. Then, Wright gently tapped on the wooden door.

Suddenly, a metal fire door at the opposite end of the hall flung open, and three assassins squared off in the hallway. A large man with a Thompson machine gun flanked by two smaller men with automatic pistols opened fire. The victims went down hard and were left in a bleeding heap on the carpet. The assassins fled the scene before anyone on the third floor was brave enough to come out of their apartment. Two of the victims were killed instantly, while Wright died shortly after in the hospital. With his dying breath, Wright told police what happened, but he could not identify the shooters. His final words were, "The machine gun worked." This was the first documented use of a machine gun in Detroit.

Crime scene investigators recovered 120 bullets from the bodies of the dead men and the splintered hallway woodwork. The third-floor residents disturbed from their sleep, dressed in robes and pajamas, were questioned by police investigators. Their stories were identical. They were awakened by the sound of automatic weapon fire, but nobody came out of their apartment until the gunmen left and they felt safe.

Questioning the Milaflores landlady, investigators discovered that apartment 308 was rented by reputed Purple Gang gunmen Abe Axler and Eddie Fletcher—Johnny Reid's former bodyguard. Investigators were interested in a wanted poster they found hanging in the apartment for New York fugitive Salvatore Mirogliotta—also known as Joe "Honey Boy" Miller—another Purple Gang member. The landlady identified the photograph on the wanted poster as "Sam Miller," who she saw frequently in the apartment. An arsenal of small weapons and ammunition was found in the apartment—twelve pistols, dumdum bullets, three shotguns, a box of shotgun shells, and several blackjacks. All that the police spokesperson would tell reporters was the victims appeared to be "underworld characters."

At 2:00 a.m. the next day, police pulled over a car with two passengers who gave their names as Harry Levine and Robert Burke, but the pair were soon identified as Purple Gang lieutenant Abe Axler and out-of-towner Thomas

Camp—a.k.a. Fred "Killer" Burke. The men were held for forty-eight hours, but no incriminating evidence was found against them. A writ of habeas corpus was served to authorities for the release the both men. Nobody else was ever brought to trial for the brutal triple murder, but it was clear to everyone who extracted the heavy price.

Charles Givens, a reporter for the *Detroit Times* observed, "Most homicides are not deep mysteries or even aggravating riddles to detectives. In nine out of ten unsolved cases, police are virtually certain who the murderers are. Proof is another thing. Question the homicide detectives who handle these so-called mysteries, and in the majority of cases, you get the same answer: 'We know who the murderer was, but there were no eyewitnesses or compelling evidence to secure a conviction.'"

The Milaflores mass shooting underscored how cunning and bold the Purples had become and what they were prepared to do to interlopers. Several former Egan's Rats gunmen found a home in Detroit as hired muscle enhancing the gang's reputation for violence and vengeance on anyone who crossed them. Fear reigned supreme in Detroit, giving the Purple Gang dominance in Detroit's underworld.

— 5 —

Fate Catches Up with Mike Dipisa

AUGUST "GUS" NYKIEL WAS a popular Detroit athlete who played semiprofessional football for a team called the Delray Merchants. When he was drafted in 1918 for service in World War I, his career as an athlete ended. When Nykiel completed his military service, he managed his family's grocery store and sponsored the Delray Merchants which competed against other football clubs from around Michigan and the Midwest. The Merchants were a semiprofessional powerhouse becoming regional champions three times in four years, and they were the team to beat in 1927. Gus Nykiel's popularity was such that a football field was named after him.

Gus and his brothers, William, Frank, and Joseph, began their rum-running career shortly after Prohibition began in the 1920s. They smuggled Canadian liquor and beer, making several trips daily in a row boat. The Nykiel brothers eventually built up a fleet of speedboats and became some of the wealthiest smugglers on the river. Their association with the Purple Gang distribution network made them rich men.

The community of Delray—on Detroit's southwest city limits—was ideally positioned for smuggling. It was across from the Zug Island channel and the Rouge River, which formed a loop in and out of the Detroit River. Boats could speed into the channel, unload their cargo to a waiting crew, and return to Canada for another load. When the Coast Guard was in pursuit, cargo in weighted burlap bags was heaved overboard and fished out later with grappling hooks. Sometimes, local boys from Delray were paid by bootleggers to dive into the river and attach a rope to their illegal cargo. It was a good way for a kid to earn some money—especially during the Depression.

On March 17, 1927, Delray speakeasy owner Gus Nykiel was arraigned in federal court for reopening his saloon at 8631 West Jefferson Avenue, which had been closed and padlocked under federal court order. Nykiel had the padlock removed and reopened his place. Several undercover Prohibition officers made buys resulting in a raid. Large quantities of beer and whiskey were seized. Nykiel was also the owner of four other places where liquor and beer was stored and distributed—8866 West Jefferson, 465 Clairpoint, 110 Henry Street, and 3021 Fourteenth Street.

Gus Nykiel was released on $5,000 bail. When his case came to trial, he pleaded guilty to violating the padlock injunction and owning the property, but he denied ownership of the liquor. He did admit he knew the liquor was stored in his business. Federal Judge Charles E. Simons fined him $1,000. The owners of the liquor were determined to be Sam Kert and Sam "Sammy Purple" Cohen—proprietors of the popular K & C Café, where politicians, police officials, lawyers, and underworld figures hung out. The two Sammies—as they were known—were under federal indictment for conspiracy to violate the Prohibition law. Both men were known mentors and senior associates of the Purple Gang. They paid their fines and walked free.

———

Nykiel's saloon was shut down permanently, but within a month, he opened a new location up the street at 8824 West Jefferson. At about 10:00 p.m. on June 27, 1928, Nykiel was parking his car in front of his saloon and scratched the paint on James Zanetti's car. Zanetti was a gunman from Chicago, hired to extort money from bootleggers and speakeasy owners in the downriver area for Pete Licovoli's Eastside River Gang.

According to Gus's brother William, Zanetti verbally abused Gus until Gus walked up to Zanetti and punched the Chicago hood twice in the face. "I'll smack you again if you come around here looking for trouble," Nykiel told Zanetti. "Tell your friends that Gus Nykiel hit you."

Zanetti and Mike Dipisa—gambler "Jimmy the Greek's" bodyguard and the man responsible for Johnny Reid's murder—returned fifteen minutes later and went into the saloon looking for Gus, finding him standing behind the bar. Dipisi said he wanted to talk to Gus outside in the street. As soon as Nykiel stepped out the door, he was shot five times at close range and fell to the sidewalk. The shooters ran for the getaway car. River Rouge Constable Edward A. McPherson happened to be in the saloon serving a patron with a summons when he heard the gunshots. With service revolver drawn, he stepped outside and exchanged gunfire, hitting Dipisa several times. For his pains, Constable McPherson was shot in the upper jaw. Passerby Mrs. Catherine Krozyck was also hit in the hand by a stray bullet.

After a short car chase, James Zanetti was arrested by two patrolmen and taken to Wayne County Jail. Twice he attempted suicide; first by beating his head against the bars of his cell and later by trying to choke himself with his belt. Zanetti was admitted to the psychopathic ward of Receiving Hospital, where he was heavily guarded and chained hand and foot to a hospital bed. Nurses reported that "at intervals, he shudders, rolls his eyes back in his head, and he quivers issuing long, drawn out moans." Psychiatrists believed Zanetti was mentally sick from "crime hysteria," or what was better known on the street as being "yellow." Dr. Polzker believed Zanetti's suicide attempt failed because he didn't have the courage to follow through with it.

Thirty-three-year-old Gus Nykiel was taken to Delray Receiving Hospital where he died from his wounds. Thirty-two-year-old Mike Dipisa was taken to Detroit Receiving Hospital, where he died from shots to the head, the back, and his right eye. Johnny Reid's killer was finally paid off in full, but Gus Nykiel's murder was the price.

When police notified Mrs. Caroline Nykiel of her husband's murder, she wept at the news. "Gus may have been a bootlegger," she said, "but he was a faithful husband and a good father."

Gus Nykiel's funeral service was July 2, 1928, at St. John Cantius Roman Catholic Church in Delray. He was buried at Holy Cross Cemetery. Hundreds of people paid their respects along the procession route. *The Detroit Free Press* reported that the majority of the mourners were women, but underworld figures and police detectives were evident among the crowd.

Gus's younger brother William told Inspector Henry L. Garvin of the crime and bomb squad that he witnessed the shooting from the front window of the saloon. At the inquest, he repeated what he saw. But Garvin thought the murder was about more than a road rage incident. The inspector told reporters he believed a grander plan was afoot—the Eastside River Gang was trying to seize control of Nykiel's business interests and control smuggling up and down the Detroit River.

At a meeting of the Wayne County Chiefs of Police Association on July 5, 1928, forty-one-year-old Constable Edward A. McPherson, who was shot in the jaw by Mike Dipisa, was recognized and awarded a platinum-finished, pearl-handled, .38-caliber Colt revolver engraved with the inscription, "He did his part to preserve the peace and dignity of the people of the state of Michigan." McPherson couldn't be there to personally accept his award. He was in the hospital recovering from facial surgery.

The Zanetti trial was slated to begin on August 30, but the prosecution's primary witness—William Nykiel—could not be found. The case was postponed twice before Detroit police announced on September 8 that their key witness was hiding out in LaSalle, Ontario, in fear of his life. The state of Michigan had no jurisdiction to extradite him. The prosecution proceeded without him. Zanetti testified, "Mike killed Nykiel. I don't even carry a gun." On September 13, James Zanetti was acquitted of Gus Nykiel's murder. After the not-guilty verdict was delivered, Zanetti and his lawyers were surrounded by backslapping and handshaking from their underworld supporters.

Gus Nykiel left his widow and seven-year-old son an estate reported to be worth $55,000—little consolation for the loss of a loving husband and father.

— 6 —

Purple Gang Gambling Rackets

WAGERING WAS OUTLAWED THROUGHOUT most of the United States by the advent of the twentieth century driving it underground but not eliminating it. When national Prohibition became law in 1920, the social phenomena of the speakeasy appeared. A speakeasy could be something as humble as a spit-and-sawdust tavern or a high-end casino-style nightclub. The high-end speakeasies catered to wealthy and well-connected Americans who considered themselves "café society" and above the law.

To attract an upscale clientele, exclusive night clubs offered a new type of entertainment called jazz music. Detroit attracted many of the country's top African American jazz performers, who provided live music so patrons could dance the Charleston and the Black Bottom—the latter dance originating in Detroit. And to appeal to women's more delicate palates, bartenders concocted sweetened drinks known as cocktails to soften the harshness of the bootleg liquor. The age of the flapper was born.

Well-dressed patrons generally sailed past a well-guarded security entrance and were shown to the main room, usually on the ground floor. If a patron's interests included wagering, a casino might be found in a back room, a second floor, or a basement. If you were known to the establishment as "all right," you would be admitted without delay. If not, the house manager would need to approve you. Depending on the clientele in the casino that night, a person might be admitted one night but not the next. Wealthy business mavens, rich industrialists, high-ranking city officials, local celebrities, and notorious underworld figures would rub elbows with alarming familiarity on any given night.

A high-end gambling establishment typically had a card room for poker, blackjack, or faro and a larger area for casino games like roulette and craps. Sports bets could be placed with a house bookie, and slot machines lined the outer walls for the wives and girlfriends of serious gamblers. Alluring women acting as "shills" (decoys) worked for the house, encouraging men to drink up and gamble more. Barmaids and cigarette girls circulated through the room carrying trays held up with neck straps. They provided gamblers with drinks, cigarettes, cigars, snacks, and chewing gum. These young women were eye candy paid to flirt with and distract male customers. Prostitutes might be found on the premise or in a nearby mob-run brothel to relieve lucky gamblers of some if not all of their ill-gotten gains. When big winners were lucky enough to leave a speakeasy unscathed, they might be rolled by street-level predators. High rollers began to hire their own personal protection.

———

Most of the Purple Gang's cash flow came from their bootlegging business, but their second-largest income producer was gambling. Abe Burnstein—patriarch of the gang—began his gambling career as a dealer and a stickman in some of Detroit's finer gambling establishments. This is where Abe networked with many of Detroit's prominent people in and out of government. He was personable and highly regarded by many of Detroit's movers and shakers. Abe was a short man and not a physical threat to anybody, but his connections helped many Purples beat raps and get out of jail. His political connections were Abe's source of inner strength.

Abe Burnstein and his younger brother Joe established their horseracing wire service in Detroit in the mid-1920s. Abe and Joe built a network of over seven hundred betting parlors in the greater Detroit area which were required to "subscribe" to their service, kicking back a percentage of their gross earnings to the Purples. Teletype operators at Western Union and Telegraph Company were paid handsomely to hold back race results from Eastern tracks and pass them along only after the Burnstein organization passed the results on to their bookies. If a horse had lost a particular race, the bookie took the bet; if the horse had won, the bookie would say the book on that race was closed. By placing their thumb on the scale, the Burnsteins were able to maximize their profits.

The Purples had another gambling sideline handled by associates who kidnapped wealthy and influential gamblers for ransom. Victims of what the press dubbed the snatch racket willingly paid to avoid bad publicity or being dumped bleeding onto a city street or drown in the Detroit River. A variation of this snatch racket precipitated the Milaflores Massacre which put the fear of God into the public and the underworld.

———

The urge to gamble was not limited to the well-heeled public and wealthy industrialists. Everyday working people wanted to wager also. If they couldn't afford to chase Dame Fortune, they were content to wink at her. Abe Burnstein realized there was a fortune to be made from the nickels, dimes, quarters, and dollars of working-class immigrants and Detroit's large minority community. Bets could be taken over the phone and winnings were tax free. What could be easier? The numbers game appealed to people who were not welcome in the high-class gambling joints of Detroit's high rollers, social climbers, and underworld figures that mingled nightly in tuxedos and evening dresses.

Purple Gang members began to take over the numbers racket throughout much of the city. For the game to run smoothly, numbers runners, bagmen, and accountants were needed to keep the money flowing. Playing the numbers gave many people in Detroit's distressed neighborhoods a steady income.

The game was easy to play—pick three numbers ranging from 000 to 999 and wait for the daily winning number. Players placed their bets with a numbers runner who would collect the money and record the bet in a handbook with the bettor's name and date of the bet written in. Each page had a serial number printed at the bottom and a receipt that the bettor used to prove they placed the bet in the event they won. The odds were one in a thousand. Bagmen collected the money from the runners and took it to a central location where a team of accountants processed the bets, counted the money, and passed on the lucre to the numbers bank. The bank was a secret location where the money was divvied up and everyone paid off. The number runners would pay the winners.

At first, the numbers were drawn from numbered balls in a ball cage or by three spins on a wheel of fortune. These methods were easily manipulated and soon fell out of favor. The Purple Gang's game was different. It used the last three numbers of the United States Treasury Department balance which was printed daily in the business section of newspapers. After anti-gambling groups complained, the Treasury Department began to round off their numbers so they wouldn't be a party to illegal gambling schemes. Not to worry, the organization easily shifted to using the three last digits of the number of shares traded on the New York Stock Exchange for the daily winning number—also found in the local papers.

Accounting books seized by Treasury agents in a raid of a numbers drop revealed that as many as six thousand men and women were employed by Detroit numbers operators. The average payout was 16 percent of the take divided among the winners. The number runners who took the bets and filled out the betting slips got 25 percent of the daily take. The bagmen who collected the money and betting slips from the bookies took them to a hidden central location. They made 10 percent of the total they brought in. Finally, the promoters took 49 percent for themselves and their overhead. All of those accountants needed to be paid. Because of the large territories where the game was played, the profits were huge.

This scheme was not without its dark side. Anyone skimming money off the top, holding out on winners, compromising the operation, or attracting unwanted attention from the authorities would be quickly eliminated. The message was clear: Transgressors could expect terrible retribution at the hands of the Purple Gang.

— 7 —

St. Valentine's Day Massacre Line Up

THE CAPONE–PURPLE GANG AFFILIATION was furthered when Capone ran out of patience with George "Bugsy" Moran and the North Side Gang in Chicago. A deadly gang war between the two Chicago gangs spilled much blood on both sides. An uneasy truce was called in the name of business between Capone and Moran. Capone continued to supply Moran's gang with bonded Canadian whiskey, but Moran soon complained the wholesale price was too expensive.

Thinking he could make a better deal with a cheaper supplier, Moran cancelled his whiskey allotment and bought his liquor elsewhere. When his customers complained about the lack of quality from his new supplier, Moran approached Capone to reinstate his allotment, but Capone had no lack of customers and made a deal with one of Moran's competitors. Capone cut Moran out of the equation and refused to resupply his organization. Unwilling to take no for an answer, the North Side Gang began hijacking shipments of Capone's whiskey after the Detroit cargo was transferred to Capone's truck drivers.

Capone was furious over the interruptions to his supply line and wanted the entire Moran Gang eliminated. Not everyone in the Capone organization wanted to resume a gang war with the North Siders. Capone's business manager and gang accountant Jake Guzik reminded Capone that blood was bad for business. Capone didn't care. Underboss Frank Nitti said the boys downtown wouldn't like it, but Capone was unmoved. Then he asked his trusted lieutenant and bodyguard Jack McGurn what he thought. McGurn narrowly escaped death after being ambushed in a Chicago hotel ten months earlier by two North Side triggermen— Frank and Pete Gusenberg. Now fully recovered, McGurn was primed for vendetta.

"While I was lying in that hospital bed, I had a lot of time to think this out, Al. Rather than hit these guys one or two at a time, we need to lure them to their headquarters on North Clark Street and take them out all at once. Then, we make it look like someone else did it."

Capone liked the basic plan, with two provisos. First, he didn't want to use any of his men in the hit squad. If they were identified, the Chicago police would be all over their organization. Second, Capone wanted to be out of town reading about the hit in the Miami papers fourteen hundred miles away. Capone gave McGurn the contract and $20,000 to set up the hit.

McGurn worked out the fine points of his plan and began putting it into action. He called Capone associate and liquor supplier Abe Burnstein in Detroit. His Purple Gang organization pulled off the Milaflores Massacre in 1927 and nobody had been arrested or tried for that triple murder. To bait the trap, Burnstein agreed to contact Bugs Moran with an offer he couldn't refuse—five hundred cases of Capone's favorite bonded Canadian liquor, Old Log Cabin, at the bargain price of fifty-seven dollars a case—fresh from the Detroit docks. If Moran could raise the cash and take immediate delivery, they would deliver the shipment. Jack McGurn calculated correctly that Moran would not miss an opportunity to stiff Capone.

For fire power, McGurn hired contract killers Fred Burke and James Ray—formerly Egan's Rat from St. Louis. Burke and Ray were freelance contract killers for hire. To assist them, McGurn hired cold-bloodied Sicilian gunmen John Scalise and Albert Anselmi, who the Capone organization used for the hit on Dion O'Banion—Moran's predecessor. All three men were morally ambivalent and proven assassins with nerves of steel.

Abe Burnstein sent three of his own men to act as lookouts from two boarding houses located across the street from the S.M.C. Cartage Company at 2122 North Clark Street. The warehouse of the shipping company was a front for the Moran gang's hangout and distribution center. This is where McGurn knew the truck would be unloaded. The Purple Gang lookouts were to keep a record of who came and went from the business for a week before the hit. Once the Moran Gang was assembled in the warehouse on the appointed day, the lookouts were to phone in the hit team. After the call was made, the trio would leave Chicago immediately and return to Detroit before a search for them could be mounted.

McGurn added one last person to the team—Joseph Lolordo wanted to avenge the murder of his older brother,

Pasqualino Lolordo, who was murdered in his home in front of his wife by the Gusenberg brothers. McGurn couldn't refuse him. Having suffered at the hands of the Gusenbergs himself, Joe was hired as the wheelman.

To sow the seeds of confusion after the murders, props were needed. The hit squad needed a police car to get the assassins to and from the cartage company. A black Lincoln was stolen for that purpose and fitted with a siren to make it look like an unmarked police car. It was hidden in a nearby garage. McGurn also needed two Chicago police uniforms to make the slaughter go as smoothly as possible. Two were purchased from a uniform supply company in the Chicago area.

On the morning of February 14, 1929, a blustery, eighteen degree wind whipped up intermittent snow flurries—Clark Street was all but deserted. The Purple Gang lookouts took their positions from their rented rooms across the street. Members of Moran's gang began drifting into the building several minutes before the shipment was to arrive. A lone man bundled in an overcoat with its collar around his ears and a fedora worn low on his head entered the cartage company. The lookouts, believing the man to be Bugs Moran, called in the hit squad. The Purple Gang lookouts grabbed their bugout bags and headed for Detroit. Their job was done.

Everything appeared to be going like clockwork. Minutes later, the phony police cruiser pulled up in front of the cartage company. Four men—two dressed as Chicago cops and two in overcoats—got out of the car and entered the building. Joe Lolordo stayed behind the steering wheel of the idling car. The counterfeit policemen armed with Thompson machine guns barged through the door separating the front office of the cartage company from the ware-house behind. The seven men waiting inside were surprised to see the police but assumed this was a routine shakedown by some rogue Chicago cops they could easily payoff.

The men were ordered to drop their guns, raise their hands, and line up with their faces against the redbrick back wall. North Side gunmen Pete and Frank Gusenberg, safecracker and mechanic James May, saloon keeper Albert Weinshank—mistaken by the lookouts for Moran—bank robber Albert Kashellek, and optician Dr. Reinhart H. Schwimmer turned their backs to the assassins.

Fred "Killer" Burke and partner James Ray dressed in police uniforms raised their machine guns. Scalisi and Anselmi entered the warehouse with a sawed-off shotgun and a .45-calibur automatic pistol. The machine guns swept back and forth cutting down the seven North Side members down while the other gunman made sure all seven men were dead. The victims were left in growing pools of blood. A German shepherd was cowering and whimpering under a Model T Ford.

The gunmen put the last part of McGurn's plan in action. Scalise and Anselmi walked out of the building at gunpoint with their hands up while the bogus policemen led them to the decoy police car that sped them away from the scene.

Several witnesses told the real police when they arrived that a squad car just left with the shooters. The bewildered officers entered the building to the frantic howling of Adam Heyer's German shepherd chained to a car bumper. The trembling dog underscored the terror he witnessed. The police entered the scene and found Frank Gusenberg crawling toward the front office, barely alive, carrying twenty-two bullet wounds. Beyond him were six slaughtered men. An ambulance rushed Gusenberg to the nearest hospital where police tried to question him while he fought for his life.

Chicago police sergeant Thomas Loftus knew Gusenberg when they were kids together. Loftus gently questioned him. "Who shot you, Frank?"

Gusenberg answered weakly in true gangster fashion, "No one—nobody shot me." Three hours later he died.

Just before the shooting, George "Bugs" Moran, Willie Marks, and Ted Newberry were walking toward the warehouse with the cash to pay for the shipment. Earlier, Purple Gang lookouts mistook Al Weinshank for Moran, as both men were roughly the same size, dressed similarly, and were easily mistaken. When Moran, Marks, and Newberry approached the cartage company, they saw the black police cruiser car in front and soon heard the rat-tat-tat of the machine guns punctuated with shotgun blasts. The three men ducked into the alley, narrowly escaping their assassins. Except for not killing Moran and not walking away with $28,500 in cash, McGurn's plan worked perfectly.

When news of the massacre spread, *Chicago Tribune* crime reporter Jake Lingle sought out Moran. "Who do you think killed your men?" Lingle asked.

"Only Capone kills like that" was Moran's answer.

But Big Al had an airtight alibi. He was in the Miami-Dade County Solicitor's office at the very moment of the massacre, answering questions about his intentions for buying property in Miami Beach. The day after the blood bath, Capone read about Moran's statement reprinted in the *Miami Herald*. When Miami reporters showed up at Capone's Palm Island villa to interview him about the massacre, he grinned and said, "The only man who kills like that is 'Bugs' Moran."

Fear and disgust gripped the public conscience. Chicago citizens demanded something be done about the wholesale killings. Suspecting Capone's triggerman Jack McGurn, the police brought him in for questioning. McGurn claimed he knew nothing about the massacre.

"I was with my girlfriend at the Stevens Hotel when the murders took place. We checked in last night at about nine and spent Valentine's Day together in bed until about three in the afternoon."

Police investigators checked the hotel register and discovered McGurn had signed in using his real name—Vincenzo Gibaldi. The Stevens Hotel desk clerk, the bellhop, and the maid all vouched for McGurn's whereabouts. Regardless, McGurn was arrested and held without bail by Chicago police to separate him from his girlfriend—the beautiful and smart-mouthed Louise Rolfe.

Louise Rolfe was the stereotypical mob moll. She showed up for the interrogation decked out in a full-length mink coat, expensive jewelry, perfect makeup, and every hair in place. After posing for press photographers—much to the annoyance of the Chicago police—Louise endured several hours of intense questioning. Rolfe held firm that she and Jack spent the entire day in bed.

"About the same time when the murders occurred," Louise said, "we were celebrating Valentine's Day with eggs benedict and champagne in bed."

Investigators were unable to shake her alibi. The press dubbed Louise Rolfe the "Blonde Alibi." She was released from police custody but placed under round-the-clock police surveillance.

McGurn was held on suspicion of underworld activity for forty-eight hours before being released on a writ of habeas corpus entered on his behalf. Before police could question Louise again, McGurn summarily divorced his estranged wife and quickly married Louise so she couldn't be forced to testify against him in court. The ploy worked.

A Chicago police investigation of the North Clark Street neighborhood where the massacre occurred brought two landladies forward who ran boarding houses across from the S.M.C. Cartage Company. Mrs. Michael Doody at 2119 North Clark Street and Mrs. Frank Arvidson at 2135 North Clark Street told police about three mysterious cab drivers who rented rooms a week before the shootings and left immediately after the murders. The women were shown mug shots and positively identified known Purple Gang members Harry Keywell, Phil Keywell, and Eddie Fletcher.

Chicago Police placed a call to Detroit crime and bomb squad Inspector Henry J. Garvin. Garvin told his Chicago brothers in blue that the Keywells and Fletcher were under police surveillance in Detroit at the time, so it couldn't be them. Inspector Garvin for some unexplained reason dismissed the Chicago inquiry. Once again the fix was in. Nobody was ever brought to trial for the St. Valentine's Day Massacre.

— 8 —

The Tide Turns

THE PURPLE GANG'S INCREASED visibility brought increased law enforcement scrutiny. On May 15, 1929, special federal agents raided a known Purple Gang hangout— the Hart Novelty Company at 8679 Twelfth Street. Twelve alleged gang members were arrested and charged by federal judge Charles C. Simons with conspiracy to violate the national Prohibition Act. They were quickly remanded to Wayne County Jail. This federal bust was meant to take as many of the Purple Gang off the street as possible, sending a message to the Detroit underworld and the public weary of the "revolving door" brand of justice that released gang members as quickly as Detroit police could arrest them. Of the twelve gang members arrested, only four were bound over for trial. The others were released for lack of prosecutable evidence.

The official charge read, "On May 10th, 1929, the defendants conspired with rum runners to smuggle beer and whiskey to the Lido Club, a cabaret located at 3747 Woodward Avenue." Alleged leader of the Purple Gang Abe

Burnstein owned the Lido. A federal judge set bail for Abe Axler, Eddie Fletcher, Irving Milberg, and Harry Sutton at $100,000 each. This was the first time Purple Gangsters couldn't make bail because the city's professional bail bondsmen refused to put up the sum of money demanded by the federal government. The federal prosecutor told reporters, "At last, we have this gang exactly where we want them."

The four defendants looked ten pounds trimmer after two months of eating Wayne County jail food. Their wives were allowed to visit them in the jail's visitation room the day before their trial. The men were confident of acquittal, but their wives feared the worst.

The trial began the next day on Tuesday, July 23. Evidence obtained by special treasury agents came from transcripts of wire-tapped telephone conversations, cancelled checks, and account books seized by federal agents. It was the testimony of James H. Taylor of the United States Navy Department's Identification Bureau that connected the signatures of Ed Fletcher and Irving Milberg with the aliases of "Eddie Fisher" and "Irving Stein" on the cancelled checks and Canadian export documents. Abe Axler and Harry Sutton were caught delivering two cases of Canadian whiskey to the Lido Club.

The case was handed to the jury on Wednesday, July 24. After only fifteen minutes of deliberation, the jury returned a guilty verdict much to the surprise of everyone. The defendants' wives could be heard weeping at the back of the courtroom. Milberg, Fletcher, and Sutton appeared shocked, while Axler took a stoic, hardline pose showing no emotion. The maximum sentence for violating the Volstead Act was two years and a $10,000 fine. The men had already served two months in county jail, so the judge sentenced them to twenty-two months in Leavenworth Federal Prison in Kansas and a maximum fine of $5,000 apiece.

After passing sentence, Judge Charles C. Simons addressed the defendants. "I don't know whether you are the hardboiled gangsters the police and the papers seem to think you are. I don't care. I don't know whether you belong to a purple gang or a yellow gang or a gang of any other color. But we are concerned here with the enforcement and dignity of the federal law. The record shows that you carried on a wholesale liquor business by smuggling whiskey into the United States and supplying speakeasies."

This was the first real law enforcement victory against the Purple Gang and their growing influence. On July 28, 1929, the four convicted Purple Gang members and sixteen other prisoners were chained hand-and-foot before they left Wayne County Jail and boarded a prison train car bound for Leavenworth Federal Penitentiary in Kansas. The prisoners were under the custody of Deputy United States Marshall George Beamer and his men.

After Deputy Beamer officially handed his prisoners over to the warden, reporters were waiting to question him about his train ride with the Purple Gang members.

"A few hours into the trip," he said, "I noticed the hardness going out of their faces—all but Abe Axler. He fought against showing any signs of nervousness. When we pulled into Chicago, I let them read the Sunday *Chicago Tribune* about the murder of their fellow gang member Irving Shapiro, shot to death just two days after their trial ended. Each man carefully read every line of the account. Afterward, they sat there quietly lost in thought. All the fight was out of them. When they saw the forty-five foot

high walls of Leavenworth Monday morning, all the prisoners were startled, except Axler, who maintained his pose of
a hardened gangster."

————

On July 27, a quiet neighborhood was rudely awakened
by the sound of gunshots. Just after 3:00 a.m., Albert Rose
of 2464 Taylor Street rushed to his window and saw a body
in the gutter in front of his house. Rose called the Detroit
police. When they arrived, Rose's neighbor Edward W.
Brown told the police he caught a glimpse of a gray touring
car speeding down LaSalle Boulevard before vanishing.
Skid marks found on the curb indicated the car swerved
and quickly stopped before dumping the body in the street.

The labels in the victim's suit had been cut out to delay
identification, but police investigators recognized the body
as twenty-five-year-old Irving E. Shapiro—a Purple Gang
extortionist and gunman. When Shapiro's pockets were
searched, he had fifty dollars in them. An expensive watch
still on his wrist indicated the motive was not robbery.
Police detectives surmised possible motives may have been
retaliation for squealing on fellow gang members leading
to their convictions, or Shapiro may have been involved in
a botched kidnapping incident and murdered by his own
gang.

The Wayne County coroner determined that Shapiro
was shot three times at close range with a .32-caliber automatic weapon. All the slugs passed through his body and
none were found. Two ejected shell casings were found on
the street. One slug entered the back of Shapiro's head and
exited through his right eye. Another shot entered his back,
crushing his spine and coming out through his chest. The

last shot to his back plowed beneath the flesh for several inches before leaving the body. The coroner believed the last bullet was fired as the body was thrown from the car into the street. Shapiro became the first Purple Gang member to be "taken for a ride." To add insult to injury, Shapiro was murdered in his new, gray touring car, which turned up three days later in a used car lot with a For Sale sign on the windshield.

Irving Shapiro was one of the top money producers for the Purples through his extortion labor racket. He muscled in on the building trades and extorted $8,000 a month from the plumbers union. Shapiro was greatly feared in Detroit's underworld and by the police despite his small physical presence. He overcompensated with ruthless violence, once gouging a man's eye out. He wore expensive suits and drove late-model luxury cars, flaunting his gains around town and making enemies. Shapiro was arrested no fewer than twenty-four times with only one conviction. Despite his extensive arrest record, Recorder's Court Judge Frank Murphy gave him only three years of probation—a slap on the hand.

Dissension in the Purple Gang's ranks resulted in Shapiro splitting off from the main mob and forming his own small crew that preyed on gamblers and vice vendors around the city. A police informer told investigators that Shapiro had threatened some Purple Gang members who he believed were cutting him short on a ransom split for the kidnapping of electrical contractor Max J. Kagan. Shapiro believed his accomplices pocketed the money and shorted him on his share. At the gang's Brewster Street headquarters, he told them, "If you don't make good, somebody's going to get hurt." Early the next morning, Shapiro's life ended in a lifeless heap on the pavement.

Another theory for Shapiro's murder was that Sam Green—alias Sam Seaman—was being shaken down for $5,000 a month by Shapiro while another Purple Gang associate, saloon owner Albert Kolski from Hamtramck, was robbed of $1,800 by Shapiro's six-man crew. Green and Kolski complained to Abe Burnstein to do something about it. Mafia businesses were getting clipped by Shapiro too. Burnstein advised Shapiro to lay off mob-protected businesses or he was on his own. Shapiro was headstrong and ignored Burnstein's warnings.

Few people mourned Shapiro's passing except his relatives. Funeral services were held on Sunday, July 28, 1929, at Lewis Brothers Funeral Parlor on 7739 John R. Street and Smith Avenue. One hundred people attended the funeral, including many uniformed policemen and detectives scattered among the mourners. When the funeral procession started for Machpelah Cemetery, only twenty people followed the pine box to its final resting place. No Purple Gang members were present. Irving Shapiro was survived by his twenty-one-year-old widow, Sophie, his three-year-old son, Bernard, and his forty-four-year-old father, Edward (Zalev), who still worked every day at his tailor shop on Alexandrine Street mourning the murder of his son.

Two days after the funeral, Ray Burnstein, Isadore Burnstein, and Joseph "Honey Boy" Miller showed up voluntarily to police headquarters at 1300 Beaubien Street to answer questions about Shapiro's shooting. Police were convinced the trio was innocent of the murder, but thought they may be able to furnish some leads. True to the gangster code, they didn't know or say anything helpful.

Police sought Abe Burnstein, who had disappeared from his customary haunts after Shapiro's murder. Investigators had information that the two men quarreled several hours before Shapiro was killed. Five days after Shapiro's murder, Abe Burnstein appeared with his lawyer, Edward Kennedy Jr., at police headquarters. He apologized for not coming sooner. Burnstein said he left Detroit for New York City on a business trip the previous Friday afternoon and didn't return until Wednesday, when he learned he was wanted for questioning about his alleged quarrel with Shapiro over independent raids on businesses enjoying underworld protection, Burnstein denied that an argument with Shapiro had occurred. Burnstein claimed he didn't know what the detective was referring to.

"Me and my brothers are old friends of Irving's. Joe and Ray went to Bishop's School with him. Irving was our pal," the Purple Gang patriarch said.

But like other Purple Gang members questioned, Abe and his brothers were contemptuously indifferent showing little interest or emotion over the loss of their longtime friend.

———————

Habitual holdups of the Mafia's nightclubs, blind pigs, and brothels continued after Irving Shapiro's assassination. One of Shapiro's crew was twenty-two-year-old gunman Zigmund Witkowski—known in Detroit's underworld as Ziggie Selbin. His specialties were robbery, extortion, and murder. Selbin was a binge drinker, mean drunk, and loose cannon. He was arrested nine times with no convictions. On one occasion while dining in a downtown restaurant, Selbin admired a man's ring and asked what he wanted for it. When the man refused to sell, Selbin clubbed him unconscious, whipped out a knife, and cut off the man's finger with the ring on it. This sort of public, mad dog behavior was bad for business.

The Purple Gang supplied lots of whiskey to Hamtramck's vice lord Chester "Big Chet" LaMare. The two organizations had a symbiotic relationship that was threatened by Selbin. After LaMare complained to Abe Burnstein about Selbin's continued holdups of LaMare's mob-protected businesses, Burnstein agreed that Selbin had to be eliminated to maintain the peace. To avoid a costly gang war, Burnstein ordered the hit.

On October 27, 1929—three months to the day after Irving Shapiro's murder—Selbin was caught on the street without his firearm. He backed into a stairwell entrance at 8833 Twelfth Street on the city's west side as an unidentified Purple Gang gunman casually emptied five shots into him. Then, the gunman turned his back and walked away with his head lowered to hide his face under his fedora.

Eyewitness Mrs. Gertrude Greenwald told police, "I just stepped off a streetcar when I saw a man thirty feet in front of me shoot the victim. The gunman slipped the gun into his pocket and calmly walked away." When asked if she could identify the gunman, Mrs. Greenwald balked, "I couldn't see the man's face because of his hat." Neither did anyone in the crowd of two-hundred gawkers who quickly gathered at the murder scene.

The recent convictions of key Purple Gang members and several internal murders created uncertainty among the ranks and threatened the Purple's leadership as the 1920s came to a close. These upheavals were only the beginning of the gang's implosion.

— 9 —

Fred "Killer" Burke Runs out of Luck

SERGEANT MAJOR THOMAS CARP developed his machine gunnery skills while serving overseas in World War I as a member of a motorcycle machine gun detachment. Carp learned to fire a submachine gun with deadly precision, and he saw lots of action. His experiences in the tank corps made him a hardened soldier with few qualms about pulling the trigger or taking a life. Upon his honorable discharge, Carp returned to St. Louis, Missouri, and worked briefly as a machinist but soon became restless. He found it easier to make a dollar working as right-hand man for Dinty Colbeck—feared leader of the St. Louis gang Egan's Rats.

Burke's criminal specialties were daring bank and armored car robberies and hiring himself out as a free-lance contract killer. In 1927, the Purple Gang needed a job done and offered Burke a contract he was only too happy to accept. Burke's longtime friend Johnny Reid—from his St. Louis Egan's Rats days—was a key Midwest distributor of Purple Gang liquor. Reid was executed in Detroit by transplanted Chicago gunman Frankie "the Pollack" Wright. The murder of Purple Gang associate Reid would not go unanswered. A trap was set. After being lured to the Milaflores Apartments at 106 East Alexanderine Avenue, Frankie Wright and his wingmen were cut down by Burke and two Purple Gang members thought to be Abe Axler and Eddie Fletcher. The three men suspected of the machine gun killings were never charged.

———

Since the Valentine's Day Massacre of seven men in a garage on Chicago's North Side, Chicago police suspected Fred Burke when an eyewitness told them she saw two Chicago policemen with machine guns lead two other men in overcoats out of the cartage company at gunpoint. She said the larger of the policemen was missing a front tooth. Fred Burke immediately came to the minds of Chicago detectives investigating the case. An all-points bulletin was issued nationwide for Burke's capture, but Burke eluded Chicago police for almost a year. He was living as Fred Dane, a fictitious Chicago feed company salesman, with his girlfriend, Viola Brenneman posing as his wife on swanky Lake Shore Drive in a $20,000 bungalow. The "Danes" divided their time between their Lakeshore Drive home and a "safe house" rented in Stevensville, south of St. Joseph, Michigan.

While driving under the influence through St. Joseph on December 19, 1929, Burke scratched the fender of George Kool's car. Kool was a cranky out-of-work farmer who engaged Burke in a heated argument. Burke threw a five dollar bill in Kool's face and sped away. Kool saw St. Joseph policemen Charles Skalay (Skelly) walking his beat and motioned for Skalay to jump onto his car's running board to apprehend Dane (Burke), whose car was stopped behind a traffic light. Kool caught up with Dane's car, and Skalay stepped off Kool's running board onto Dane's. Wanting to keep his real identity hidden, Burke took a .45-caliber automatic pistol and shot the twenty-four-year-old policeman in the stomach. As Skalay slid off the running board, Burke shot him again in the left side and once more when he was lying on the pavement.

Burke power shifted his car and sped south down US 12 (Michigan Avenue). State police were only minutes behind. After fifteen minutes of pursuit, police found Burke's car in a ditch with two of its wheels sheared off by a telephone pole. Burke lost control when his car hit an ice patch and skidded off the road. Michigan state troopers carefully approached the car with guns drawn, but Burke was gone. Immediately after the wreck, Burke flagged down a motorist, commandeered his car at gunpoint, and drove to Paw Paw, Michigan. Burke ditched the car on a side street and went into a dance hall for a drink. There, he hired a young man to drive him to an undisclosed location where the trail went cold. Once again, Burke eluded police.

Meanwhile, state troopers searched Burke's wrecked car and found a receipt from a St. Joseph lumberyard. Lumberyard owner Frank Cupp told police he knew Fred Dane, who the police thought they were seeking. Cupp said Dane was a wealthy oil man who was remodeling a bungalow outside of town. A state police unit was immediately dispatched to the Dane house where they found thirty-five-year-old Viola Brenneman posing as Mrs. Dane. The lead investigator asked Mrs. Dane where her husband was. Suspiciously evasive, Mrs. Dane wanted to know why they were looking for him.

"Your husband is wanted for murdering a police officer."

Mrs. Dane said he could not possibly be the man they were looking for. Her husband was in Chicago on business and not expected to return until Monday. Against Mrs. Dane's protests, investigators went to the second floor and found an arsenal of weapons in a bedroom closet including two Thompson submachine guns, two automatic sawed-off shotguns, two high-powered deer-hunting rifles, seven automatic pistols, eleven tear gas bombs, and several bottles of nitroglycerin. When confronted with the cache of weaponry, the fictitious Mrs. Dane shrugged. "I don't know anything about those guns. My husband is a businessman."

"What business is your husband in, Mrs. Dane?"

"He's a salesman for a Chicago feed company."

"He's not a rich oilman?"

"Not that I know of," she answered.

Detectives searched through a chest of drawers and found men's shirts with the monogram FRB that led them to the realization they were actually in pursuit of Fred Burke.

Next, the detectives went into the basement where a growling German shepherd kept them at bay. Mrs. Dane got the dog and chained him outside. Investigators searched through a storage cabinet and found nine hundred rounds of .45-caliber machine-gun bullets, two canvas sacks of pistol and shotgun cartridges, four bulletproof vests, and twenty gallons of homemade wine. On the top shelf of the cabinet, Michigan State Police hit the jackpot. They found $319,850 in negotiable bonds from a five-man robbery of Farmers and Merchants Bank in Jefferson, Wisconsin, on November 7, 1929.

Mrs. Fred Dane was taken into police custody for receiving stolen property. She was soon revealed to be divorcée

Viola Ostroski Brenneman, who had a fifteen-year-old daughter away at private school. Brenneman had paired up with Burke in the summer of 1927, some eighteen months before.

———

When St. Joseph authorities realized they were dealing with Fred "Killer" Burke, a phone call was placed to the Chicago police notifying them they had discovered a cache of Fred Burke's guns, including two Thompson submachine guns. The Chicago police asked if someone could deliver the guns to Northwestern University's newly established scientific crime detection laboratory. The St. Joseph prosecutor drove the weapons to Chicago to personally deliver them.

Chicago residents and the Chamber of Commerce were tired of the bloodletting on their city streets. It damaged the city's reputation and was bad for business. With major funding provided by the Chicago-based Colgate-Palmolive-Peet Corporation, federal government crime grants, and Northwestern University alumni, the first modern forensic crime lab in the nation was established. A group of wealthy Chicago businessman traveled to New York City to persuade Lieutenant Colonel Calvin H. Goddard—the nation's foremost expert in the new science of ballistics—to head their state-of-the-art facility.

Calvin Goddard began his pioneering work on ballistics as an ordinance officer during World War I and continued his research at the New York City Ballistics Bureau making him a nationally recognized authority. His groundbreaking work established that every gun and bullet shot from a gun has distinct and unique markings. Each part of a gun's firing mechanism leaves a unique signature on the cartridge and the bullet. The lands and grooves in the barrel imprint distinctive ridges on the sides of the bullets. The firing pin indents the primer cap, and the gun's breech imparts concentric circles on the base of the cartridge. No two guns leave identical markings. Slugs and bullet casings found at crime scenes are compared to test bullets fired from a recovered firearm into a water tank recovery receptacle. The test slugs are recovered and compared to crime scene slugs with a specially designed comparison microscope.

Goddard's first mission in his new position was to dispel rumors that the Chicago police were complicit in the St. Valentine's Massacre. All eight Thompson submachine guns in the Chicago police arsenal were test fired into the recovery receptacle and compared against bullets taken from the bodies of the victims. None of the test bullets matched. Chicago police were cleared of any involvement in the massacre.

The news that Burke's machine guns were recovered excited Chicago ballistics experts. On Wednesday, December 18, 1929, after comparing bullets from two of the victims, Goddard and his team of forensic investigators established that test slugs fired from Burke's Thompson submachine guns matched bullets found in the victims' bodies. Burke's machine guns were linked forensically to the St. Valentine's Day murders.

Detroit police had long suspected Burke was the machine gun wielding assassin in the Milaflores Apartment triple homicide on March 27, 1927. Test bullets were brought to Detroit for comparison with slugs and cartridges removed from that crime scene. Once again, they matched. Chicago and New York police also suspected Burke of killing New York crime boss Frankie Yale on behalf of the Capone organization. Bullets from Yale's body were carefully packed and shipped to Chicago for examination. Ballistics experts announced on Friday, January 17, 1930, that one of Burke's machine guns was proven to be the murder weapon.

Three of the most notorious murders of the Roaring Twenties were connected to Fred "Killer" Burke, prompting Chicago authorities to release this statement to the press: "Fred 'Killer' Burke is the worst desperado in this country since Jesse James. He is responsible for over twenty cold-blooded murders and a string of high profile bank robberies throughout the Midwest. Burke is wanted by federal authorities and eight states. Rewards amounting to almost $100,000 are offered for his arrest and capture. He is armed and dangerous and should be approached with extreme caution."

———

Fred Burke seemed to vanish into thin air again until Thomas Bonner—a small-time booze and narcotics racketeer acquainted with Burke through mutual friends—was seen wandering out of the Grand Rapids Police Department on Wednesday afternoon, July 9, 1930. Bonner needed some cash and planned to give Burke up for the reward money, but Burke was tipped off by someone in the know. In a desperate act, Burke burst into the Bonner home just after midnight on Thursday, July 10. Without a huge expense of words, Burke announced he knew Bonner was a police informer and shot him squarely between the eyes. Then Burke drove off, leaving Mrs. Bonner in shock with her five-month-old son shrieking into her ears. Later that day, she formally identified Burke from a mugshot photo as her husband's killer.

For three months, Burke lived with a young blond woman named Carolyn in a rented summer cottage on secluded Hess Lake, thirty-two miles north of Muskegon, Michigan. The cottage was owned by William Smith, who had ties to the illegal brewing industry as a wholesaler of raw materials such as corn syrup, yeast, hops, whole grains, and wort. Burke paid Smith well and in cash for the rental of his summer cottage and his discretion.

Smith dropped by the cottage for a visit on Sunday, July 13, 1930, to collect the rent and make sure everything was going well. Burke said they needed some groceries. It was a nice day, so Smith walked rather than drove to the nearby general store to pick up a few things for his tenants, who were understandably hesitant about being seen in public and identified. When Smith arrived at the country store, he saw a heavily-armed police contingent milling around the parking lot.

Smith went inside to pick up some groceries and cigars for Burke. While shopping, he overheard the Newaygo County Sheriff explain over the pay phone what was holding up their operation. A squad of Chicago detectives hadn't arrived on the scene yet. It was clear to Smith who the police were after. He waited for an opportunity and stuck his neck out. Smith called Burke to tip him off. The fugitive and his blond girlfriend grabbed what they could and jumped into Smith's Ford, leaving Burke's brand-new Packard behind. Burke and Carolyn drove past the country store while the raiding party was in the general store's parking lot getting their orders. Minutes later, the renegades were on the open highway speeding away.

At 6:00 p.m., the police posse finally took up their positions surrounding the cottage and slowly closed in.

Burke's flashy Packard was parked near the front door. The Michigan State Police captain in charge called out on a megaphone, "This is the Michigan State Police. The cottage is surrounded. There is no escape, Burke. Come out with your hands up, so nobody gets hurt."

Slowly a screen door creaked open as the police cocked their weapons and steadied their aim. An elderly woman in an apron came out with her hands up.

"Anybody else in there, Ma'am?" Asked the startled police commander.

"No. They left half an hour ago."

"Then who are you?"

"I cook and keep house for Mr. and Mrs. Campbell."

Against all odds, Burke eluded the posse and got away again, but the raid was not a total loss. Left behind were a sawed-off shotgun, a rifle, and twenty gallons of whiskey and beer. The cook was released after questioning, but when ownership of the cottage was established, William Smith was arrested and held for questioning by police. Burke's Packard was impounded and checked for fingerprints. Burke's prints were there, as were his lady companion's, but hers were not on record, so police were unable to identify her.

———

Burke's next move was to head to Missouri to hide out under the alias of Richard F. White. Somewhere along the way, he ditched the blonde, or she wised up and left him. Burke then met naïve, twenty-year-old Bonnie Porter, and the couple was soon married in Centerville, Iowa, on June 17, 1930. Bonnie knew Burke as Richard White—a wealthy oil broker who often traveled on business. Burke hid out for almost eight months as Richard White in his father-in-law's ramshackle farmhouse in Green City, Missouri. Rather than buying and selling oil leases, Burke returned to bank robbery. The more he kept his gangster activities in the shadows, the easier it was for him to maintain the front of a respectable businessman masking the dangerous reality of his underworld life. But mob life and family life have a tendency to bleed together, and there is always a price to pay.

As dumb luck would have it, crack police work wasn't what brought Fred Burke to justice. Burke was recognized by Green City gas station attendant Joseph Hunsacker, who saw Burke's photo in *True Detective* magazine while reading an article on the St. Valentine's Day Massacre. Hunsacker recognized the man as oilman Richard White. After giving the matter some thought, Hunsacker contacted the FBI. They suggested he contact the St. Joseph, Michigan, police department. Hunsacker went immediately to the railroad station and sent a Western Union telegram.

Four St. Joseph policemen promptly jumped in an unmarked police car and drove to Green City, Missouri, where they joined the local sheriff and a rural constable. The posse waited until 6:00 a.m., when Sheriff Hoover rapped on the farmhouse door and flashed his badge at Barney Porter, Burke's father-in-law. The gun wielding St. Joseph detectives swept past Porter. Burke was taken as he slept in a first-floor bedroom next to an open window in case he had to make a quick escape. Captain Lard stepped between the bed and the window. A loaded automatic pistol lay on the seat of the chair next to Burke's bed. Lard quietly pocketed it.

Sheriff Hoover pushed the bed frame with his boot, startling Burke awake. He woke up to the site of four burly men with their weapons drawn. Burke feared they were gangsters out to get him and insisted on seeing their identification. When Burke saw their police badges, he appeared relieved. Police found $765 in Burke's pants.

Burke's wife, Bonnie, was visiting a girlfriend in Kansas City and not present for the arrest. When Bonnie was found, she was apprehended and questioned about her husband's activities. Bonnie insisted she knew nothing of her husband's real identity or his criminal past. She thought Burke was a wealthy oilman who traveled a lot. The young woman convinced investigators that she had no idea whom she had married. Since the gangster's wife is often unaware of the true source of her husband's income, the money comes in unquestioned and goes out the same way.

After some jurisdictional squabbling between Illinois and Michigan prosecutors, it was agreed that the killing of Patrolman Charles Skalay in St. Joseph was the strongest case against Burke. The hardened criminal was pleased because Illinois was a death penalty state and Michigan was not. Burke was extradited and driven 568 miles guarded by a police caravan to St. Joseph, Michigan—a fifteen-hour drive. When Burke arrived in St. Joseph, he was placed in the old redbrick Berrien County Jail under heavy guard at 8:15 p.m. He was arraigned the next morning on Monday, March 30, 1931 before Berrien County Magistrate Joseph Collier on a charge of second-degree murder in the killing of St. Joseph Policeman Charles Skalay on December 14, 1929.

Michigan authorities wanted to remand Burke to Jackson State Prison to prevent an attempt on his life or a breakout engineered by his gangster friends. The Berrien County Jail didn't seem strong enough to hold a man like Burke. But he refused the prison transfer which was his right as a defendant. Burke said he had a falling out with the Purple Gang, and Jackson prison was full of convicted Purple gangsters. Burke knew he wouldn't last a month there.

On Monday, April 27, 1931, Fred Burke was led from the jail to the courthouse in handcuffs. At 2:30 p.m. Burke surprised everybody at his arraignment by pleading guilty to second-degree murder. Judge Charles E. White sentenced Burke to life in prison at hard labor to be served in Marquette Prison in Michigan's Upper Peninsula. When the judge asked Burke if he had anything to say, Burke replied, "Thank you."

The four St. Joseph policemen involved in Burke's capture hoped to split the reward money but were informed they were disqualified because they were paid law enforcement officers on duty. But to show their gratitude, the St. Joseph Board of Commissioners awarded Captain John Lard, E. R. Kelley, A. W. Thedinga, and Melvin Sweptson a two-week paid vacation for their part in the capture of desperado Fred Burke.

Burke was driven to Michigan's high-security Marquette Prison with a heavy state police escort. For almost nine years, he worked as a foreman in the leather goods department at the prison. His prison record was clean, and other inmates regarded him highly. Early morning on Wednesday, July 10, 1940, Fred Burke died in bed from a massive heart attack at the age of forty-seven. Burke's wife—twenty-nine-year-old Bonnie—failed to attend her husband's funeral but learned she would inherit a sizeable portion of his considerable net worth after the probate court settled his estate.

When a big-shot gangster dies, a woman often pays the price by exchanging her life of gilded luxury for hard knocks and obscurity. Bonnie Porter was lucky in that regard. She landed on her feet.

—10—

Law Enforcement House of Cards

ONE OF THE MOST notorious Detroit policemen of the Prohibition era was Inspector Henry J. Garvin. He joined the force in 1914 and became a detective in 1918. By 1923, he rose to the rank of detective-lieutenant and was appointed to the criminal investigation squad by Police Commissioner William P. Rutledge. By 1928, Garvin was appointed head of the newly formed crime and bomb squad investigating the Cleaners & Dyers War. It was Garvin who boasted to the press that he was "the gent" who was responsible for naming the Purple Gang. He was the self-avowed enemy of organized crime in Detroit, and he investigated many of the city's most notorious and ghastly gangland murders.

Driving to headquarters in an unmarked patrol car at 7:30 a.m. on January 2, 1930, the thirty-nine-year-old inspector was ambushed by three gunmen dedicated to his demise. Gunfire shot out the rear window of the patrol car Garvin was driving. A bullet grazed his neck. The pursuit car pulled alongside Garvin's vehicle and sprayed its side with automatic pistol and shotgun fire forcing the car to swerve to the curb before the assassins sped away. Garvin was hit in the neck, left arm, and torso before slumping onto the bench seat.

———

Golden-haired, eleven-year-old Lois Bartlett, walking on her way to Keating School, was hit by stray shotgun pellets meant for Garvin. Two neighborhood women—Mrs. J. S. Tolton and Miss Clara Laird—were the first to reach the Bartlett child lying bleeding on the snow-covered sidewalk. Miss Laird carried the young girl to her home. All Lois could tell police investigators was that she heard shots and felt a couple of burning pains. Then, she collapsed. Lois was rushed by ambulance to the same hospital Inspector Garvin was taken to. Emergency room doctors found shotgun pellets in Lois's body—one in her upper body, two in the arm, and one in the back of her head lodged near her spinal cord which was life-threatening. Crime scene investigators found twenty-nine bullet and shotgun pellets embedded in the porch and exterior of the house where Garvin and Bartlett were shot.

———

When a policeman falls or is wounded in the line of duty, the brotherhood marshals its forces and goes after the culprits. But Garvin was considered a rogue cop who had made enemies on both sides of the blue line. Someone wanted Garvin dead, and police investigators thought they might know who.

Eight members of the Joe Moceri/Pete Licavoli Belle

Isle gang were immediately arrested but released for lack of evidence. Moceri and Licavoli were arrested on Saturday—two days after the attack. Both men denied any knowledge of the shooting and offered their condolences to Inspector Garvin. Later that day, they were released after convincing Inspector Sprott they were not involved in the assassination attempt.

Concurrently, Detective Adolph Van Coppenolle of the Black Hand squad told police commissioner William P. Rutledge that Inspector Robert "The Scotsman" MacPherson had plotted against Garvin to have him "taken out." Van Coppenolle asserted there was bad blood between the rival inspectors and that MacPherson had asked him to arrange with underworld figures to have Garvin assassinated. When rumors of the plot leaked to the press, Commissioner Rutledge refused to say whether he would order a police board investigation of the incident which caused a feeding frenzy with the press. The *Detroit Free Press* headline on January 11, 1930, jumped off the front page: "Police Smoke Screen Veils Scandal in Garvin Shooting."

When Henry Garvin was questioned from his hospital bed about the allegation, he was indignant about the bickering going on over this departmental squabble and adamant there was no connection between the underworld attempt on his life and the police department.

"It was gangster enemies who shot me," Garvin said. "The attack was instigated out of revenge. I saw the trigger-men but didn't recognize them—probably from out of town. I don't attribute the attack to my fight with Joe Moceri or his gang. The story that I lost $400 to Moceri during an all-night poker game in Jim Bond's speakeasy is a lie. Any one of several gangs in this city might have made this attack on my life. I've been warned through underworld sources time and time again."

When asked about Van Coppenolle's rumor that the shooting was instigated by a jealous colleague within the department, Garvin indignantly refused to honor the question with a response.

Police Commissioner Rutledge passed the matter over to Superintendent James Sprott, who told the press that he looked into the matter and found "there was nothing to it." Van Coppenolle was questioned by his superiors and denied that he leaked such a statement to the press. "These rumors are a bunch of hooey," Rutledge said.

———

Meanwhile, a shotgun pellet that endangered Lois Bartlett's life was removed from the base of her skull. A spokesman for Receiving Hospital told reporters that the eleven-year-old was recovering nicely. Her mother added, "I spend night and day at my daughter's bedside. She is all my husband and I have."

Eleven days after the shooting, Detroit Superintendent of Schools Frank Cody visited Lois in the hospital awarding her a promotion certificate from sixth grade level B to sixth grade level A. The conscientious student was worried about missing schoolwork since she had been in the hospital. The visit was intended to relieve Lois's concerns and rest her mind about promotion. She thanked Superintendent Cody for the certificate.

"I am glad I passed," she said.

———

On January 15, a photo opportunity was engineered

for the press by Police Commissioner Rutledge. Inspector MacPherson went to Inspector Garvin's bedside to shake hands and exchange pleasantries to dispel any rumors of bad blood between them.

Four days later, the police commissioner announced at his weekly press briefing that Detective Van Coppenolle was removed from the Black Hand squad and sent to patrol "the sticks" for making an erroneous statement that a rival inspector had ordered him to solicit gunmen to "bump off" Garvin. Rutledge surmised, "Detective Van Coppenolle's statement may have been the result of an emotional disturbance to a greater or lesser degree. Under department questioning, the detective reversed his story, clearing Inspector MacPherson of any wrong-doing."

The same day that Commissioner Rutledge threw Van Coppenolle under the police wagon, Inspector Garvin left the hospital to recover in the comfort of his home. Lois Bartlett was still confined to a hospital bed.

On Friday, January 24, 1930, more than three weeks after her shooting, Lois Bartlett was able to sit up and receive some school friends at her bedside for the first time. Lois spoke of her desire to see her Persian kitten Snowball. Gathered around her in the hospital room were a brightly colored French doll, a plush dog, and a bowl of goldfish the police had given her. Lois said she spoke with Inspector Garvin over the telephone and told him she was happy he had recovered enough to go home and expressed gratitude for the many flowers he had sent her.

———————

Public outcry and pressure from the press could be sidestepped no longer. Commissioner Rutledge announced,

"Van Coppenolle will be tried by an internal police tribunal on charges of conduct unbecoming an officer and making false statements about other members of the department to the detriment of such members." Then Rutledge resigned his commission over health issues and retired. Newly elected police commissioner Harold H. Emmons took over the chairmanship of the police board trial at Superintendent James Sprott's request. "So there can be no basis for a complaint of prejudice of any kind, it would be better if someone who was not so close to the picture sat on the board." Mayor Bowles and police department officials wanted to clear the air as soon as possible and place this scandal behind them.

The police board hearing began on Friday, February 7, 1930. Van Coppenolle testified under oath before the board and the assembled press: "The things I'm about to tell you will mean certain death for me," Van Coppenolle began. "I was contacted sometime before October 20th by a kidnapping ring who promised they would turn kidnapped David Cass over to me once he was ransomed—telling me I should come to room 2612 in the Book-Cadillac Hotel if I wanted more information.

"My partner Sergeant Arthur Pieper and I cautiously approached the apartment and heard loud talking from within. I knocked and someone inside said 'Shush,' then asked, 'Who is it?' I said 'Buff'—my nickname on the street. The door opened and we walked in. Four men pointed pistols at us. I told them to relax and put their guns on the bed, which they did. I went into the back room with their leader to talk in private while Sergeant Pieper waited for me in the front room. As we were leaving, I told Pieper, 'I think we can get the Cass boy back alive.'

"But something went terribly wrong. The boy was found

murdered two days later. Then, the kidnapping ring accused their go-between—Inspector Garvin—of double-crossing them and pocketing the money. I was told to tell Garvin if he didn't come clean, his days were numbered."

Commissioner Emmons asked why Van Coppenolle and Pieper didn't call for some reinforcements to arrest the men at the Book-Cadillac Hotel.

"Because commissioner, you understand what happens to a police officer who double-crosses a gang which has taken him into their confidence. I'd be marked lousy and then I'd be dead. I was still hopeful I could get Cass back."

"Did you tell Garvin?"

"I informed him immediately, and he snapped back, 'Who told you that?' I answered I didn't know. They were from Chicago's Moran gang as far as I could gather."

"How did you determine that, Van?"

"Because one of the men mentioned he would have been found dead on the warehouse floor if it weren't for taking his mother out for breakfast on St. Valentine's Day. Another of the guys called his wife in Chicago, and a man answered. When his wife came to the phone, he asked her, 'What's the plumber doing there at this time of night?'

"Angry, he told his wife he'd be home in a couple of days when his work in Detroit was done. Then, he hung up and turned to me explaining he was leaving in a few hours by plane to catch his wife and the plumber together."

Members of the police hearing board suppressed their amusement. The story sounded like a clumsy attempt by the kidnappers to conceal who they were and where they came from by implicating the Moran gang in Chicago.

"Let's get back to Inspector Garvin. What happened next, Van?"

"The next day, Garvin called me into his office, telling me two boys in the Black Hand squad told him the Scotsman (Inspector MacPherson's nickname) had arranged to have him bumped off. 'I want you to tell the commissioner what you told me. You owe it to me.'"

"I told Garvin I didn't want to. I was afraid I would lose my job. Garvin told me not to worry. 'I'm in good with the governor and I'll protect you,' he said.

"Garvin made an appointment for me to see Commissioner Rutledge the next day in this very room. The commissioner told me to speak in whispers despite being the only people in the room. 'I understand,' Rutledge said, 'you have some information that Inspector Garvin is to be bumped off.'

"'Yes,' I said. 'He's going to get it.'

"'Well, I have information from several sources telling me that you conspired to kill him. If Garvin gets it, you'll be blamed. Don't be a fool. Who told you he would get bumped off?'"

"It became clear I was being put in the middle. I told Rutledge I had spoken to Garvin and McPherson. 'You know the Scotsman and Superintendent Sprott are like this,' he said, crossing his fingers. 'Before I leave this department, I'll discredit McPherson.' Then he added, 'Mum's the word.' I didn't know who to trust. A month later Garvin was attacked and my story was leaked to the press. Now the press calls it a 'prophesy.' I never made such a prediction."

"Do you deny making any such statements?" Commissioner Emmons asked.

"I agreed to deny what I told my superiors in confidence just to put an end to the controversy and take the dark cloud off the department. Then, Inspector Fred Frahm called me in and asked if I'd be willing to go to the psychopathic ward at Receiving Hospital for some tests. 'For what?' I asked. 'Commissioner Rutledge thinks you may be emotionally unsettled,' Frahm said."

"Did you refuse?"

"It was clear I was being set up as a department scapegoat. I went home and talked it over with my wife. She said it would cast a shadow over her and our kids. She would rather have me quit my job rather than do that. If I did anything of that sort, she would take the kids and leave me. When I told Superintendent Sprott and Inspector Frahm the next day that I refused, Sprott called me a 'yellow dog.' I said back to him, 'At least I'm not a rat.'"

When Van Coppenolle was dismissed from his testimony, his partner Sergeant Pieper was called as a witness and verified Van Coppenolle's account about the visit to the Book-Cadillac Hotel in October. Pieper had nothing new to add. He was there to back up his partner.

Commissioner Emmons asked, "Don't you outrank Coppenolle?"

"Yes, sir."

"Then why didn't you take the lead role?"

"Because this was Coppenolle's case, and I didn't want to interfere."

Up next to testify was former Commissioner Rutledge, who had resigned from the force two weeks prior to the hearing over health concerns. His replacement, Commissioner Emmons, asked Rutledge why it took him two months of delays before he addressed the issue. Rutledge detailed how he'd had an operation for goiter, taken trips to Washington and Chicago on police business, and dealt with his responsibilities in the "Fernandez case."

"Please tell this trial board what Detective Van Coppenolle told you about this matter."

"Van Coppenolle related to me that Inspector MacPherson had taken him for a ride in a patrol car and asked him to arrange for some 'wops' to have that 'son-of-a-bitch' Garvin bumped off." The rest of Rutledge's testimony was vague and convoluted leaving the trial board and the press with a muddled view of what was said and what was done.

When the proceedings were adjourned for the lunch recess, Van Coppenolle was mobbed by photographers outside the board room. After the flashbulbs nearly blinded him, he said, "That's enough, boys," waving them off. As Van Coppenolle stepped into the stairwell, Garvin rushed and slammed him against the wall. For his trouble, Garvin broke his arm—the same one recently shattered by a bullet in his shooting. Because of intense pain, Garvin was rushed to Receiving Hospital to get his arm reset. After the altercation, Van Coppenolle gladly posed for the press photographers to take more pictures for their evening editions.

Because of intense pain after his altercation with Van Coppennolle, Henry Garvin chose to remain a patient in Receiving Hospital rather than attend the police board's afternoon hearing. When the hearing resumed, Detective Sergeant Max Waldfogel of the Black Hand squad was called to testify. Rather than testify against Van Coppenolle, Waldfogel linked Inspector Garvin with the kidnapping racket in Detroit, which changed the focus of the hearing.

"The kidnapping of racketeers, gamblers, and wealthy Jewish businessmen was unknown in Detroit before the formation of Garvin's crime and bomb squad in 1927," he said.

"That's quite a statement. What makes you think there is a link?" Commissioner Emmons asked.

"Garvin's name keeps coming up in these kidnapping cases. Jewish businessman Gerson C. Cass—father of slain kidnap victim David Cass—believes Garvin was responsible for the murder of his son. I spoke with Mr. Cass in his lawyer's office located in the Dime Building. He told me he was having more trouble with the kidnappers after paying $20,000 in ransom. They demanded $10,000 more, but Cass refused to go to the crime and bomb squad. He told me, 'I'm through with Garvin. I know he was in on the kidnapping plot.'"

"That's hearsay, Sergeant Waldfogel. Do you have any proof?"

"I'm just telling you what I heard."

"Do you know anything about the Jackie Thompson kidnapping?"

"Yes, I was in the Black Hand office upstairs the night Jackie Thompson was released. Former Commissioner Rutledge was there also. I heard Mr. Thompson tell Rutledge, 'I'm surprised you have a man like Garvin working for you. He almost got my boy killed.'

"Thompson said he received a phone call and was told his child would be returned in a couple of days once the ransom was paid. He informed Garvin, and the next day the story was all over the newspapers. Then Thompson got a message saying, 'Now, you double-crosser, the next time you open your mouth, you'll get your baby's head back in a box.' A barber named Owen Jackson offered to help Thompson recover his son, but Garvin arrested Jackson before he could help, and jeopardized the life of Thompson's son."

Waldfogel told the hearing board, "I have had direct or indirect information regarding every Jewish kidnapping case over the past nine years of service with the Black Hand squad. Most people connected with the victims believe Garvin to be the head of the kidnapping gang."

"That's very disturbing, Sergeant. Didn't Garvin have any oversight?"

"Commissioner Rutledge established the crime and bomb squad and placed Garvin in charge giving him free reign to handpick his own men."

"To whom did he report?"

"No one."

"Do you have anything else to add?"

In another damaging Garvin disclosure, Waldfogel said, "The Rappaport brothers—known bootleggers—were arrested and charged by Garvin's crime and bomb squad for the cold-blooded murder of Purple gangster Irving Shapiro. Garvin's men brought the brothers in for a perp walk. The press photographers snapped photos for their evening editions reporting the Rappaports as suspects in the Shapiro killing—a known Purple gangster. The brothers told me a mysterious bail bondsman approached them in jail, offering to get them out of trouble for $4,000 and insure they had no further trouble with Garvin or his crime and bomb squad. They refused and were released from jail twenty-four hours later on a writ of habeas corpus. I wasn't looking for information on this case; they sought me out."

Commissioner Emmons wanted to know if the Rappaport brothers would agree to come in and testify before the hearing board the following week. Sergeant Waldfogel said he thought they would. Then, he was dismissed from the stand.

What started as an internal affairs investigation and an inquiry into Van Coppernolle's "conduct unbecoming an officer" mushroomed into an investigation of alleged scandal at the highest levels of the Detroit Police Department. After Wayne County Prosecutor James E. Chenot read the transcripts from the first day's proceedings, he issued this statement to the press on Sunday:

"At the trial of Van Coppenolle, I gather the hearing is developing into more than that. When charges are bandied about to the effect that police officers are committing crimes or aiding and abetting criminals, I, as county prosecutor, immediately become interested. I intend to be present as a participant for the rest of this hearing."

Rather than focus on the behavior and fitness for duty of Adolph Van Coppenolle, the subject of the police inquiry became Inspector Henry J. Garvin. Two members of Garvin's squad were slated to give testimony at Monday's hearing—detectives William DeLisle and Roy Pendergrass. DeLisle took the stand first and testified that he had been a member of Garvin's squad since its inception in 1927. Prior to that, he had been a member of MacPherson's Black Hand squad.

Commissioner Emmons began the questioning. "Do you remember arresting a group of Purple gangsters on December 16, 1929?"

"Yes, sir."

"And you charged them with carrying concealed weapons?"

"Yes, sir."

"Did you make a report to that effect?"

"Yes, sir."

"Did you sign the report?"

"No, I dictated it to a stenographer."

"And was that report subsequently changed?"

"I turned the report over to Inspector John Reid and another was written."

"Who made the new report?"

"Inspector Garvin."

"Please recount what occurred on the night of December 17, 1929, Detective DeLisle."

"My partner Roy and I were patrolling when we saw five men come out of the Addison Hotel at 10:00 p.m. and get into a Cadillac sedan. We recognized the Burnstein brothers, so we slowly approached their parked car. We asked them to get out of the car which they did. I saw Ray Burnstein take a gun from his pocket and place it on the floorboard before he got out. The rest of the men were carrying concealed weapons. Joe Burnstein had a loaded .32-caliber Smith & Wesson revolver; his younger brother Isadore Burnstein was carrying a loaded .32-caliber Savage automatic; Jules Joffa had a loaded .32-caliber Smith & Wesson revolver; and Joe Miller was packing a .32-caliber loaded Colt automatic pistol. All of these men had police records, and they were driving a car that belonged to Charles Jacoby—an associate and brother-in-law of Abe Burnstein involved in the Cleaners and Dyers War."

"Were they ever tried?"

"Not to my knowledge, sir."

"Who released them?

"Judge (Frank) Murphy of Recorder's Court."

"Who ordered an amended report written?"

"I understood later that Garvin changed it."

"Do you know why it was changed?"

"Garvin told Roy and me that former Mayor Smith

wanted the case dropped. 'Those are my orders and your orders too,' Garvin said."

DeLisle's testimony was the most damning and volatile yet for Garvin because it linked him directly to the falsification of a police report and the release of known criminals on an actionable charge. Pendergrass corroborated his partner's testimony.

Commissioner Emmons was outraged. "Here is a case where records were falsified, the prosecutor was misled, and criminals were released from custody and protected against prosecution. You say it was all done because Garvin ordered it?"

"That's what I said."

"Did you sign the report?"

"No. Our names were typed at the bottom."

DeLisle and Pendergrass were experienced detectives and produced copies of the original report and the amended report. They presented the documents to the hearing board, entered as exhibits A and B.

When Pendergrass was on the stand, Emmons asked if Garvin ever directed him to lay off the Purple Gang. "No" was his reply.

Emmons turned to Wayne County Prosecutor James E. Chenot. "Jim, I want a warrant swore out for these five Purple Gang members to be brought up on charges of illegally carrying concealed weapons."

The court was dark on Wednesday because of Abe Lincoln's birthday holiday. Garvin sent word from his hospital bed to the hearing board that he was too weak to respond to allegations made against his reputation. "Rather than send a lawyer to represent me, I will defend myself in my own way. If I am ordered to appear tomorrow," he said, "they'll have to take me on a stretcher. My mind is active, but my body is weak."

Thursday's session found former Mayor John W. Smith bursting into the hearing room, vehemently denying that he ordered Inspector Garvin to release five Purple Gang members on concealed weapons charges. On the stand, Smith demanded that a twenty-four member grand jury be convened to investigate all angles of the current Detroit Police Department scandal.

Next called to the stand were six witnesses to the poker game that allegedly ended in a brawl between Garvin and members of the Eastside River Gang on November 26, 1929. The witnesses stood on their constitutional right against self-incrimination refusing to testify. That line of testimony was a dead end for the police trial board.

The bell captain and bellboy at the Book-Cadillac hotel were called next to testify whether they remembered a group of five or six people having a late-night party in room 2612. Both men said they see so many guests daily that they didn't remember anything about those men—except they didn't look like businessmen. The combined testimony of the bell captain and the bellboy had no value to investigators.

Former Commissioner Rutledge was recalled to the stand and asked by Commissioner Emmons about the release of the five Purple Gangsters while he was in charge.

"Were the five men released from custody under any special order or dispensation that permitted them to carry weapons?" Emmons asked.

"Not to my knowledge," the former police commissioner answered.

"Then there is no reason why these men should be allowed to carry concealed weapons on their persons?"

"None, whatsoever."

"When you learned that two different reports existed for the arrest of these known criminals, why didn't you investigate which report was correct?"

"I'm wondering that myself. I can't believe that I didn't, but I have no record to show I did." Then the former commissioner began rambling testimony about random transfers, promotions, power struggles, and other workplace melodrama involving Superintendent Sprott and Chief of Detectives James E. McCarty and others.

When Superintendent Sprott was called to the stand, he testified that former Mayor John C. Lodge asked him to remove Inspector Garvin from the crime and bomb squad. Sprott claimed that Mayor Lodge called him about rumors charging Garvin with protecting and associating with criminals.

"Lodge told me he would be pleased if Garvin was removed. It blew over and nothing ever came of it. Garvin continued his heavy-handed tactics unaccountable to his superiors."

That prompted an angry denial from Lodge, who asserted in the newspapers that he never requested Sprott— then superintendent of police—to remove Garvin from his post. "I never ordered any police officer either discharged or promoted."

Other highly placed police officials were called to the stand, but the more they tried to explain themselves and rationalize their actions, the more corrupt or incompetent they appeared. Charges, denials, and countercharges were heaved back and forth, causing internal bleeding within the police department's leadership.

Commissioner Emmons knew he had lost control of

the hearing and searched for a way to shut down the proceedings to stop the hemorrhaging of the department. The headline in the *Detroit Free Press* evening edition read, "Each Accuses the Other of Untruths as Trial Board Goes Deeper into Police Investigation."

When the last witness was called, Commissioner Emmons made a statement to the press justifying not calling Harry Garvin back to the stand. "Garvin is a sick man. It is not the policy of this department while I'm here to kick a man while he is down. No further steps against him are contemplated at this time." Then, Emmons brought the gavel down.

The police board trial ended, and an internal report was issued on February 19, 1930. Adolph Van Coppenolle was demoted and reassigned to patrol a beat on the northern outskirts of the city far away from police headquarters. His punishment was a fifty-dollar reduction in monthly pay linked to his demotion and the cancellation of his leave days.

After the hearing, Wayne County Prosecutor Chenot issued a statement, saying, "It must be pointed out that the trial board is in no sense a judicial tribunal. It is mainly an instrument to maintain discipline within the department. As a consequence, the ordinary rules of evidence enforced in a court of justice were not adhered to. Witnesses were permitted to testify to vicious hearsay, rumor, suspicion, interference, and innuendo, all of which are inadmissible in any court. This hearing was called to determine the truth of Detective Van Coppenolle's allegations and not to slander or implicate other officers.

"That said, the public thinks the Detroit Police Department is corrupt from top to bottom. The public perception will taint any jury, making it almost impossible to get a conviction that depends upon the testimony of the police. This is a tough break for the policeman walking a beat who is honestly seeking to give the public protection. We are doing everything possible to rid the city of these criminals."

The Wayne County Circuit Court refused to call a grand jury to investigate further into the Garvin shooting. One week after the Van Coppenolle hearing, Recorder's Court Judge Henry S. Sweeny dismissed the resuscitated possession of concealed weapons charges against Raymond Burnstein, Isadore Burnstein, and Joseph "Honey Boy" Miller, who appeared in court. The charges were also dropped against Joseph Burnstein, who was said to be in California, and Jules Joffa, who was serving time in an Ohio penitentiary.

Purple Gang attorney Edward J. Kennedy Jr. asked that the evidence about the confiscated weapons be suppressed on the grounds that the search and seizure was illegal. There was no probable cause. The judge's decision to dismiss the concealed weapon charges kept the slate clean for the Purple gangsters. Although their arrest records were extensive, none of them had ever been convicted—except Jules Joffa.

The last vestige of former police commissioner William P. Rutledge's domination of the Detroit police department was wiped out in a terse order by new commissioner Harold H. Emmons on March 11, 1930. The order read: "The crime and bomb squad is hereby abolished effective March 15th, 1930."

Superintendent Emmons began his institutional housecleaning. The Garvin squad was split up among various squads, and seven veteran inspectors were relieved of duty through retirement in an attempt to stop the bleeding within the department. Retirees were given a $2,000 retirement bonus, and upon their death, their families would receive a $2,000 death benefit. The crime and bomb squad was replaced with a vice squad with jurisdiction over prostitution, gambling, bootlegging, and speakeasy operations. A holdup squad was created to handle all cases of robbery.

Inspector Garvin was rumored to be retiring soon. Police department physicians said Garvin's wounds would make it dangerous for him to continue as a policeman as his disabilities were permanent. Under retirement rules, a policeman disabled in the line of duty may be retired without consent if his disability continues for a period of six months. Garvin's six months would have been over July 2, 1930, but one day short of automatic retirement, Garvin returned to work. Police physicians now declared Garvin physically fit to return. His only duty was to find the men who shot him and bring them to justice—something he was never able to do.

Garvin held onto his post for nine more years until another department shakeup over a gambling scandal eliminated three inspectorships. Garvin agreed to quit the force after serving twenty-five years. He and three other district inspectors were first demoted to inspectors which lowered their annual salary from $5,740 to $4,180. Then, they were entitled to one-half of their salary as retirement pay. To supplement his income, Garvin went into a partnership with two other men and bought the San Souci bar and restaurant on Harsen's Island.

Henry Joseph Garvin—long feared and hated by Detroit's underworld and victim of a near-fatal shooting by gangsters—was found dead of a massive stroke in his bedroom at 8:30 a.m. on Saturday, May 8, 1943.

In a July 20, 1958, *Detroit Free Press* feature story entitled "And Whatever Happened to the Little Girl Cut Down by a Gang's Guns," Lois Bartlett Alford was interviewed by journalist Riley Murray. Thirty-nine-year-old Lois lived with her husband and son at 4184 West Point Street in Dearborn Township. She told Murray that the city of Detroit paid for her five-week stay at Receiving Hospital, and the police passed the hat giving her a gift of $256.

"That's despite the fact that my surgical and medical bills since I was discharged from the hospital have cost us nearly $3,000. Shotgun pellets affected my eyesight, hearing, and my arm making it hard for me to pick up anything heavy. Nine years ago, I underwent abdominal surgery to remove more pellets."

Lois Alford said she believed the city should have a pension fund for unfortunate victims like her. "Something like this might happen to you," she added. "The pleasantries and flowers and all were nice at the time, but they don't do me any good now."

Mrs. Alford passed away on December 28, 2001, and was buried in Parkview Memorial Cemetery in Livonia, Michigan, at the age of eighty-three.

Fig 1: Detroit Skyline in 1929 with Windsor, Ontario in the foreground. The forty-two story Penobscot building was Detroit's tallest skyscraper until the Renaissance Center opened in 1977. Source: *Walkerville Publishing*

Fig 2: Detroit/Windsor Funnel editorial cartoon. Source *Walkerville Publishing*

Fig 3: Last Call. Source: *Walter P. Reuther Library, Archives of Labor and Urban Affairs, Wayne State University*

Fig 4 Man on Canadian Booze Holiday postcard. Source: *Walkerville Publishing*.

Fig 5: Prohibition fleet preparing to go out on patrol. Source: *Walkerville Publishing*

Fig 6: Bootleggers caught on camera by Detroit News photographer Monroe D. Stroecher hiding in a coal elevator at the foot of Riopelle Street. Source: *The Detroit News*

Fig 7: 1925 Ford Model TT stuck in Lake St. Clair ice. Notice the onlookers wearing ice skates. Source: *Walter P. Reuther Library, Archives of Labor and Urban Affairs, Wayne State University*

Fig 8: Smuggler waiting for the "All Clear!" signal from across the Detroit River. Source: *Walkerville Publishing*

Fig 9: United States Customs Agent modeling the latest in 1928
Prohibition fashion. Source: *Alarmy Photo*

Fig 10: Customs agent wearing vest harness. Source: *Walter P. Reuther Library, Archives of Labor and Urban Affairs, Wayne State University*

Fig 11: Booklet playing on parents' fears that their daughters would be debauched by rumble seats, hip flasks, and the Charleston. Source: *Lutes Casino in Yuma, Arizona*

Fig 12: Detroit police pour beer into sewer.
Source: *The Detroit News*

Fig 13: Detroit Police beer bust. Source: *Google Images*

Fig 14: Canadian freight train car adjacent to an export dock. Boats would pull up, show their export papers, and be loaded in short order often returning many times a day.
Source: *The Windsor Star*

Fig 15: Airplane liquor smuggling attracted little customs attention providing a steady source of bonded Canadian liquor for the Capone organization. Source: *The Windsor Star*

Fig 16: Federal agent padlocking a speakeasy.
Source: *The Detroit News*

Fig 17: Customs agents at work. Source: *Walkerville Publishing*

Fig 18: Tommy Gun magazine advertisement.
Source: *Google Images*

Fig 19: Tools of the Prohibition trade. Source: *Google Images*

Fig 20: 1932 Ford Phaeton Police Cruiser. Notice the bullet deflector protecting the car's radiator. Source: *Walter P. Reuther Library, Archives of Labor and Urban Affairs, Wayne State University*

Fig 21: Detroit Free Press Prohibition Sunday feature with
graphic illustration. Source: *The Detroit Free Press*

Fig 22: Early Purple Gang round up photo hiding their faces with their fedoras. First row: Abe Burnstein, Irving Milberg, Harry Keywell, and Joe Miller. Second row: Ray Burnstein, Simon Axler, Eddie Fletcher, Abe Axler, and Irving Shapiro. Source: *Walter P. Reuther Library, Archives of Labor and Urban Affairs, Wayne State University*

Fig 23: 1928 Purple Gang round up photo, looking defiant. Abe Axler seated, standing Simon Axler, Eddie Fletcher, Sam Goldfarb, Phil Keywell, Abe Zussman, Willie Laks, Harry Fleisher, and Jack Stein. Source: *Walter P. Reuther Library, Archives of Labor and Urban Affairs, Wayne State University*

Fig 24: Sam Kert and Sam "Sammy Purple" Cohen were Purple
Gang liquor distributors who owned the high-end K & C Café
where politicians and underworld figures mixed freely.
Source: *Google Images*

Fig 25: Abe Burnstein 1920 mugshot.
Source: *Walter P. Reuther Library, Archives of Labor
and Urban Affairs, Wayne State University*

Fig 26: Joe Burnstein mugshot. Source: *Walter P. Reuther Library, Archives of Labor and Urban Affairs, Wayne State University*

Fig 27: Ray Burnstein mugshot. Source: *Walter P. Reuther Library, Archives of Labor and Urban Affairs, Wayne State University*

Fig 28: Isadore "Izzy" Burnstein mugshot. Source: *Walter P. Reuther Library, Archives of Labor and Urban Affairs, Wayne State University*

Fig 29: Irving Milberg mugshot. Source: *Walter P. Reuther Library, Archives of Labor and Urban Affairs, Wayne State University*

Fig 30: Irving Shapiro mugshot. Source: *Walter P. Reuther Library, Archives of Labor and Urban Affairs, Wayne State University*

Fig 31: Abe Axler. Source: *Walter P. Reuther Library, Archives of Labor and Urban Affairs, Wayne State University*

Fig 32: Eddie Fletcher. Source: *Walter P. Reuther Library, Archives of Labor and Urban Affairs, Wayne State University*

Fig 33: Fred "Killer" Burke. Source: *Google Images*

Fig 34: Harry Keywell. Source: *Walter P. Reuther Library, Archives of Labor and Urban Affairs, Wayne State University*

Fig 35: Phil Keywell. Source: *Walter P. Reuther Library, Archives of Labor and Urban Affairs, Wayne State University*

Fig 36: Abe Axler and Eddie Fletcher with their lawyers. Source: *The Detroit Times*

Fig 37: Purple Gang on way to County Jail. Handcuffs were welded to a long chain. Source: *The Detroit Free Press*

Fig 38: Purple Gang on trial for the Collingwood Manor Massacre. Source: *The Detroit Times*

Fig 39: Police Commissioner Harold Emmons. Source: *The Detroit Free Press*

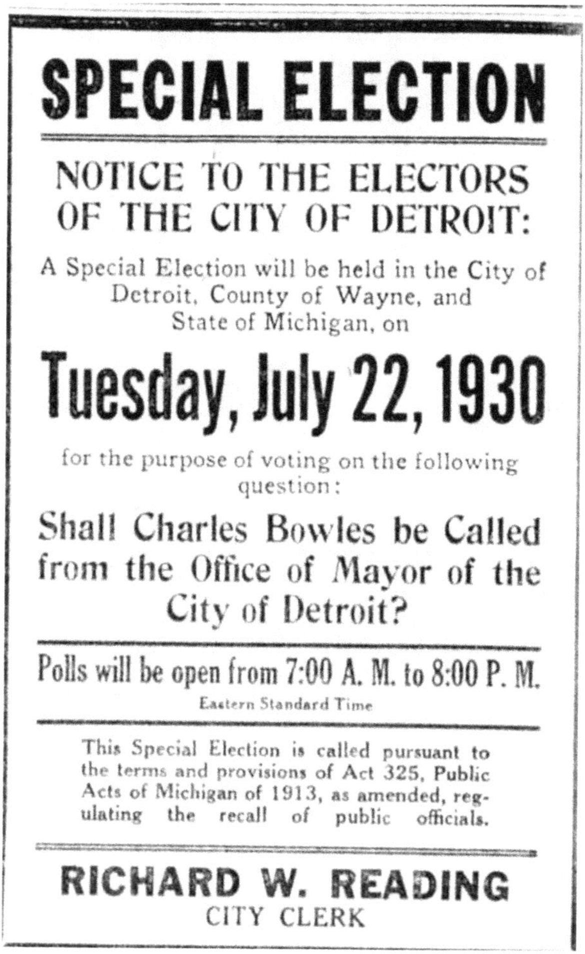

SPECIAL ELECTION

NOTICE TO THE ELECTORS OF THE CITY OF DETROIT:

A Special Election will be held in the City of Detroit, County of Wayne, and State of Michigan, on

Tuesday, July 22, 1930

for the purpose of voting on the following question:

Shall Charles Bowles be Called from the Office of Mayor of the City of Detroit?

Polls will be open from 7:00 A. M. to 8:00 P. M.

Eastern Standard Time

This Special Election is called pursuant to the terms and provisions of Act 325, Public Acts of Michigan of 1913, as amended, regulating the recall of public officials.

RICHARD W. READING
CITY CLERK

Fig 40: Mayor Bowles Special Election.
Source: *The Detroit Free Press.*

Fig 41: Mayor Charles Bowles.
Source: *The Detroit Free Press*

Jerry Buckley: He won a crusade, but lost his life.

Fig 42: WMBC radio
commentator Jerry Buckley.
Source: *The Detroit Free
Press*

Fig 43: Harry Millman mugshot - 1928.
Source: *Walter P. Reuther Library, Archives of Labor and Urban Affairs, Wayne State University*

Fig 44: Harry Millman mugshot – 1937.
Source: *Walter P. Reuther Library, Archives of Labor and Urban Affairs, Wayne State University*

Fig 45: Millman's car. Police investigators believed seven to ten sticks of dynamite were used to blow up Millman but a valet became the unintended victim. Source: *Walter P. Reuther Library, Archives of Labor and Urban Affairs, Wayne State University*

Fig 46: Millman's LaSalle from the passenger side. Source: *Walter P. Reuther Library, Archives of Labor and Urban Affairs, Wayne State University*

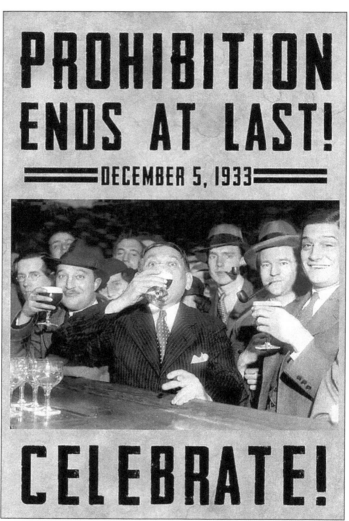

Fig 47: Prohibition Ends. Source: *Google Images*

—11—

Joseph Burnstein Cheats Death

Harry Kirschenbaum ran a small printing shop as a front for the Purple Gang's wire service, providing Detroit's seven hundred betting parlors around town with daily horse racing information. All bookies were required to "subscribe" to the gang's handbook operation or be put out of business permanently. Joseph Burnstein depended on Kirschenbaum to keep the operation running smoothly. Kirschenbaum would have been good at the job were it not for his love of the opium pipe which interfered with business. The handbook needed daily management, and Kirschenbaum would go missing for days at a time. Joe Burnstein eventually lost his temper with his friend and burst into Kirschenbaum's home to knock some sense into him.

"Where is he?" Burnstein demanded from Mrs. Kirschenbaum.

"Harry's not at home, Joe."

Burnstein knew better. The smell the opium was hanging thick in the air.

As Burnstein bounded up the stairs, Mrs. Kirschenbaum said, "Harry's been on a six-day binge, Joe."

"I'll take care of it."

Kirschenbaum heard Joe climbing the stairs and grabbed his German Lugar automatic pistol. As Joe burst through the door, Harry shot him in the gut. Joe stumbled down the stairs and fled from the house. He ran down Cortland Avenue the best he could with Kirschenbaum firing his pistol at him when the Lugar suddenly jammed. Burnstein collapsed in front of a grocery store. Thinking Burnstein was dead Kirschenbaum threw the pistol in the bushes and returned to his home for another pistol before fleeing in his automobile.

Local miniature golf operator George G. Barrett saw Kirschenbaum shoot Burnstein and throw his pistol aside. Barrett retrieved the firearm and cleared the jam. He jumped in his car and pursued the shooter. Kirschenbaum shot at Barrett through the rear window of his car while Barrett returned fire. The high-speed chase lasted fifteen blocks until Barrett took a slug in the chest and was forced to pull over. Kirchenbaum disappeared.

Joe Burnstein was rushed by ambulance to the hospital with a spleen injury. Had it not been for quick medical attention and a supply line of Purple Gang blood donors, Joe would have died. It took two complete transfusions. Meanwhile, Joe's wife, Marguerite, was still in the hospital after giving birth to their first child only the week before. When the attempt on her husband's life occurred, Abe Burnstein made the decision not to tell Marguerite right away which drove a wedge between him and her.

On the day of the shooting, Kirschenbaum fled Detroit and headed for Los Angeles where he was arrested weeks later. The Detroit police searched Kirschenbaum's home and found a stash of opium and drug paraphernalia. Kirschenbaum was arraigned in absentia with two counts of felonious assault for attempted murder. The feds also charged him with possession of a controlled substance. Police investigators discovered Harry Kirschenbaum was a New York hoodlum brought to Detroit six years before to act as a bodyguard for "big shots" in the gambling syndicate. Arrested eighteen times in New York, he served four prison terms—two of them in Sing Sing. If convicted in either case, Kirschenbaum would be behind bars for a very long time.

Mrs. Kirschenbaum, when questioned on the scene, told police that Burnstein and her husband were business associates, but she didn't know any details about the business they were in. When Joe Burnstein was questioned in the hospital, he refused to bring charges against Kirschenbaum to avoid self-incrimination and being labeled a squealer.

Homicide Inspector John Navarre told reporters there were two possible motives. "The shooting may have been a sudden, homicidal, drug-begotten frenzy, or it may have been a dispute over the city's handbook racket."

The other shooting victim—George G. Barrett—did press charges for assault with intent to kill against Kirschenbaum. To dodge a subpoena to testify, Burnstein hid out in Canada, but Judge John A. Boyne issued a bench warrant for him. To avoid arrest, Burnstein appeared the following day in Recorder's Court with Purple Gang lawyer Edward Kennedy Jr.

Dressed in a brown sport coat, white linen pants, and an orange tie, the Purple Gang boss testified he suffered a blow on the head that prevented him from remembering who shot him. "I was invited to Harry's home because he was having marital problems. I helped him and his wife out before. That's all I remember until I woke up in the hospital."

Kirschenbaum's defense attorney Rodney A. Baxter—an occasional Purple Gang lawyer—argued that Burnstein was trespassing in his client's home, and Barrett was unjustified in chasing Kirschenbaum and shooting at him. His client shot back in self-defense.

The case was handed to the jury on Friday, August 15, 1930. A panel of eight women and four men deliberated for three hours before delivering a not-guilty verdict. Judge Boyne made a point of telling the jury, "This is your verdict—not mine." Kirschenbaum was remanded to the custody of federal officers to be tried on narcotics charges. In that case, he was found guilty and given a stiff federal prison term.

George G. Barrett was incapacitated and unable to work for a time as a result of his wounds and filed a lawsuit against Joseph Burnstein in Common Pleas Court on Monday, October 5, 1931, for $500 to pay his hospital bills. Barrett claimed that Joe Burnstein promised to pay Barrett's doctor bills but he was never reimbursed. The case was settled out of court when Burnstein's lawyer handed Barrett an envelope containing five crisp one-hundred dollar bills.

———

Joseph Burnstein had a talent for business and became a wealthy man overseeing the Purple Gang's gambling and bootlegging concerns as well as several legitimate enterprises. He owned the Kibitzer Club speakeasy, a three-chair barber shop, a clothing store, an auto parts store, and oil wells in Mt. Pleasant, Michigan. A newspaper marriage notice was run in Marguerite Ball's hometown of Kenosha, Wisconsin. It listed Joe as vice president of the Detroit Motor Company (DMC), but this was impossible. Joe was born in 1899 and Henry Ford dissolved that company in 1901 after it failed.

His businesses acted as fronts for the gang and vehicles for laundering gang money. For his showgirl bride, Joe bought a Tudor-style mansion for $100,000 in the exclusive Palmer Woods neighborhood at 1920 Lincolnshire Drive. From outside appearances, Joe Burnstein looked like a prosperous businessman, but unlike legitimate businessmen, he owned a custom-built, armored Cadillac driven by a chauffeur who doubled as his bodyguard like Al Capone did in Chicago.

Despite the wealth and privilege Joe's notoriety brought, his wife, Marguerite, gave Joe an ultimatum: "Either leave Detroit and the gang, or say good-bye to me and your daughter." Joe followed her to California, where he lived off his investments and became a gambling consultant to California and Nevada gambling concerns. Joe and Marguerite remained married for almost fifty-five years until Joe died in California from heart disease in 1984 at the age of eighty-four.

—12—

The Arthur Mixon Murder

July 22, 1930

Detroit speakeasies and blind pigs were notorious for the harsh quality of their whiskey. Only the Purple Gang's best customers paying top dollar like Al Capone would receive full-strength, bonded Canadian liquor. What product they couldn't smuggle across the Detroit River, they hijacked. To increase their supplies and profits, it was standard practice to cut the genuine article for their less-discriminating customers.

A cutting plant was an easy operation to set up. Used bottles were collected and rinsed but never sterilized. Next, the good stuff was split up into three bottles. High-proof medicinal alcohol or white lightning from neighborhood stills was diluted with water to reach the approximate 80 proof of the original. Coal tar extract or some other coloring agent was added to achieve the proper amber tint, and flavorings were added to cut the harshness. Last, counterfeit labels and revenue stamps were attached to make the bottles look authentic. With no quality control, the final product could make users sick or blind. Some people died from contaminated "doctored" booze and others suffered from "shaky leg" (tremors). That was of no concern to the Purple Gang—large profits were their only motivation.

The Purple Gang operated several such plants around the city, but a cutting plant hidden in an old barn within the gang's territory at Hendrie Avenue and Hastings Street showed what lengths the gang would go to protect their secret plants. On July 22, 1930, Purple gangsters Morris Raider, Philip Keywell, and Harry Millman were busy cutting liquor when they heard something outside the barn. The three men were jumpy and quickly looked to see what made the sound. A Negro teen had lifted a hinged barn window and looked in. The gang feared he was spying on them and might come back with friends to steal their liquor or rat them out to police.

Raider and Keywell chased the seventeen-year-old ice peddler and confronted him in an alley. Raider and Mixon exchanged heated remarks before Morris Raider told twenty-one-year-old Phil Keywell, "Let's put him on the spot!" The alley echoed with three gunshots that pierced Mixon's back as he tried to escape. The shooting was witnessed by four of Mixon's friends who scattered. The gangsters rushed to the barn, locked it up, and fled the scene. The next day, Keywell and Raider were arrested by Detroit Police, while their partner Harry Millman, who hadn't participated in the shooting, went scot-free.

The state of Michigan tried the men separately in Recorders Court. Phil Keywell was charged with premeditated murder and tired first. After the case went to the jury, the foreman told Judge Thomas M. Cotter they were hopelessly deadlocked after sixteen hours of deliberations. When it was discovered that four of the jurors were tainted by associations with the Purple Gang, Judge Cotter declared a hung jury and tried Keywell again with a new panel. This time, the second jury returned a guilty verdict. On October 21, 1930, Philip Keywell was sentenced to life in prison without parole.

Two weeks later, Morris Raider stood trial for manslaughter. Raider claimed he was in Canada with cabaret singer Margaret Gernaey at the time and had two witnesses to support his alibi. The jury chose to believe Mixon's friends who were eyewitnesses to the killing. Three of them identified Raider as the man who chased their friend and told Keywell, "Let's put him on the spot." Raider declared that he was innocent and maligned. He accused the Negro eyewitnesses of giving perjured testimony at the direction of the prosecutor and the police.

After six and a half hours of deliberation, the jury returned a manslaughter conviction on Friday, November 13, 1930. Before Raider was sentenced by Recorder's Court Judge John V. Brennan, he addressed Raider: "With your intelligence and education, Mr. Raider, you should have known better than to become involved with gangs. I hope when you emerge from prison you will have learned your lesson and will direct your energies into worthwhile channels."

Defense lawyer Edward Kennedy Jr. announced to the judge, "I've sent affidavits to the Michigan Supreme Court, in which all three of the eyewitnesses state the Detroit police forced them to designate Raider as the killer." The judge was unmoved. He sentenced Raider to twelve to fifteen years in state prison.

The conviction of Keywell and Raider marked the first

break in the wall of immunity the Purple Gang enjoyed throughout the 1920s whenever they were brought before the courts. With the recent federal convictions for violating the prohibition laws—Abe Axler, Eddie Fletcher, Irving Milberg, and Harry Sutton serving time in Leavenworth federal prison—Detroit police believed they had broken up the Purple Gang. Some police openly doubted the existence of the Purples. They felt the catchy name was given to a group of young men who were more or less loosely knitted together from time to time in doubtful enterprises but no longer a serious threat to Detroiters.

—13—

The Italian Crosstown Mob War

May 31, 1930–February 6, 1931

WITH THE DEATH FROM pneumonia of Mafia kingpin Sam Catalonotte on February 14, 1930, a power vacuum developed among the various Italian gangs in Detroit. The struggle to be *capo de capi* ("boss of bosses") erupted into a bloody gang war when West-Side crime boss Chester (Cesare) "Big Chet" LaMare attempted to ambush and murder six Mafia dons in one fell swoop to become Detroit's unchallenged godfather.

LaMare was one of the local Mafia's top money earners who believed he deserved to be Capo Régime. LaMare operated many illegal downriver Detroit enterprises under the aegis of his Westside mob. LaMare claimed as Westside territory the city of River Rouge at the mouth of the Rouge River extending south to Grosse Isle. The long shoreline offered refuge for bootleggers, and the island geography provided many places to hide at night. Once the cargo made it across the Detroit River, the booze needed to make it past the real danger—the hijackers. LaMare and his associates did not take poaching by independent smugglers lightly. If you were lucky, all you lost was your haul. Some truckers weren't so lucky.

LaMare ran an extensive alky-cooking ring in Wyandotte while ruling as undisputed vice lord of Hamtramck to the northeast of his home base. Hamtramck is a city enclosed on all sides by Detroit with a Chrysler plant as its financial anchor. If anyone wanted to do business in Hamtramck, they needed to pay LaMare tribute in the form of a kickback. If businessmen refused, they could suffer a beating or death depending on how big an impression Big Chet wanted to make. Holdout businesses might be burned down, stench bombed, or dynamited out of existence. LaMare ruled his territory with an iron fist.

In 1929, Ford Motor Company's security czar—Harry Bennett—gave LaMare a lucrative contract to supply Ford's massive Rouge Plant with food concession stands. As long as LaMare refrained from labor racketeering, he was given a free hand. The business was a moneymaker and a great way to launder racket money. Soon, he set up a distribution center for gambling and narcotics activities within the plant. The operation was such a success he was able to buy a Ford dealership in Wyandotte.

But rather than go legit—LaMare felt the time was ripe for an underworld power play. Headquartered in the Venice Café, Big Chet had a crew of fifteen men, including feared mob enforcer "Black" Leo Cellura. Big Chet began poaching on Joe "Uno" Zerilli's east side bootlegging and narcotics territory. Zerilli was the leader and the brains of the Eastside River Gang. Zerilli and his crew began to push back.

In an uncharacteristic display of diplomacy, LaMare invited Detroit's Mafia chieftains to a fish market restaurant at 2739 East Vernor Highway for a conference to settle differences and avoid bloodshed. Joe Zerilli, his brother-in-law Bill Tocco, and the other Mafia dons smelled a rat and didn't attend. Instead, they sent Gaspare "the Peacemaker" Scibilia (a.k.a. Gaspare Milazzo) with his lieutenant Sam "Sasha" Parino to reconnoiter the café. The two elder Mafiosi showed up as scheduled at noon on Saturday, May 31, 1930. They took seats at a table in the back of the restaurant and ordered lunch.

LaMare's gunmen rushed into the restaurant and opened fire on the men with .32-caliber automatic pistols; then they briskly walked through the kitchen escaping into the alley. Scibilia's career as a peacemaker ended in a hail of bullets. His wingman Parino was hit four times and died in Receiving Hospital at 2:30 p.m. without revealing to police who shot him. Parino did tell investigators before he died that there were two gunmen.

Mafia boss Joe Zerilli's lieutenants—William "Black Bill" Tocco and Angelo Meli—swore a blood oath to get LaMare and his henchmen. The Fish Market Murders—as they were called—ignited the bloodiest gang war in Detroit's Prohibition history with over twenty gangland murders occurring in Detroit and downriver Wyandotte. When Zerilli's bodyguard Angelo Meli found out that Westsiders Joe Amico and Joe Locano were the triggermen for the Scibilia and Parino hit, he sent word to the two Joes that unless they put LaMare on the spot, they would die in his place.

"Big Chet" LaMare—unsettled that his treachery was

exposed and incomplete—beat a hasty retreat and went into hiding in New York City hoping to avoid the retribution that would surely come. With their boss out of town, "Black" Leo Cellura and several other LaMare loyalists saw the writing on the wall and switched their allegiance to Angelo Meli's crew. The balance of Mafia power in Detroit shifted to the Eastside River Gang.

Police investigating the Fish Market Murders found two witnesses—John Kimmel and Edmund Ruttenberg—who saw the killers leave through the alley after the shooting. Both men were taken to police headquarters and shown mugshots of local Italian mobsters. Separately, the witnesses identified Joe Amico and Joe Locano as the gunmen. The Westside gangsters went into hiding.

Acting on an anonymous tip two months later, police apprehended Amico and Locano in a raid on the home of Joe Catalonotte at 808 Rivard Boulevard in Grosse Point. Police armed with machine guns and tear gas prepared to storm the house when gunmen Joe Amico stuck his head out an upstairs window and threatened, "I'll shoot the first copper who tries to enter the house."

Reserve forces were brought in to quickly surround the property. The Michigan State Police deputy commissioner threatened to shoot up the house if the men refused to surrender. Joe Catalonotte—not wanting to see his home destroyed—ordered the men inside to surrender. Catalonotte, Elmer Macklin, Joe Locano, Baggio Bonconotti, and Joe Amico were arrested. The five men were held separately at different police precincts around the city to make it difficult for mob lawyers and bail bondsmen to spring them all at once.

Joe Amico and Joe Locano had outstanding murder

warrants for the Fish Market Murders and were held without bail as they were proven flight risks. A search of the raided house produced a shotgun, five pistols, and a large cache of ammunition. Ballistics tests showed that none of the confiscated weapons was used in the Fish Market Murders.

The Scibilia and Parino murder trial began on Friday, October 17, 1930, in Detroit's municipal Recorder's Court. Both prosecution witnesses suffered from memory loss on the stand and were no longer positive Amico and Locano were the men they saw the afternoon of the murders. To further compromise the prosecution's case, the defense produced a surprise witness—Benjamin "Bennie the Ape" Sebastiano, who was managing the fish market the afternoon of the murders.

The prosecutor asked Sebastiano, "Are you affiliated with either of these defendants?"

"What do you mean?"

"Have you ever done business with them?"

"Yes."

"In what capacity?"

"As manager of the restaurant, I'd see they got a good table and good service."

"Did you seat Scibilia and Parino the day of their murders?"

"No."

"Why not?

"Because they came into the place and seated themselves in the back."

"What about Mr. Amico and Mr. Locano? Were they in the restaurant too?"

"Yeah, they were talking with the owner—Philip Gaustello—in front of the restaurant when two men rushed into the cafe and opened fire on Scibilia and Parino. The shooters ran out the back door."

"Were you able to recognize either of them?"

"Only from their backs."

"Then you can describe what they were wearing?"

"Not exactly, everything happened so fast. When the shooting began, everyone hit the deck. Then the shooters were gone."

The prosecution rested and the defense never called their clients to take the stand in their own defense. The judge gave the case to the jury on Thursday, October 23. After deliberating for less than six hours, they acquitted Amico and Locano. Both men were released to freely roam Detroit city streets for the first time in three months. That night, a reception was thrown in their honor by some of the boys in Greektown at the Grecian Gardens restaurant.

———

Beginning with the fish market murders of Gaspare Scibilia and Sam Parino on May 31, 1930, bodies starting piling up all over town.

On July 7, Sam Gaglio and his brother Joe—two small-time bootleggers—were shot by LaMare gunmen with sawed-off shotguns, while gassing up their car at a filling station on 6320 Mack Avenue.

The next murder was well-known Westside gangster Sam Cilluffo on July 12. He was shot with a volley of bullets by two LaMare gunmen while sitting in his car in front of 1380 East Jefferson Avenue.

Two days later on July 14, Westside hood Henry Tupancy was shot in his car on Field Avenue by a St. Louis hitman imported as the triggerman.

Two days after, on July 16, Purple Gang hijacker Donald Overstein was shot several times and left to die in an alley off Huber Avenue.

The La Salle Hotel lobby murder of popular Detroit radio commentator Gerald Buckley on July 23 resulted in the calling of a grand jury to investigate crime conditions in Detroit.

On July 31, hijacker and liquor runner Philip Robertson was shot to death at Fourth Avenue near Michigan Avenue.

Two weeks later on August 14, booze trafficker Gennari Mongistani was taken for a ride because of a hijacking double-cross.

On August 22, William Butler was shot near Brooklyn Street and Alexandrine Avenue after hijacking a load of Eastside liquor.

Sicilian John Campari was shot dead on August 23 in front of 3732 Riopelle as a vendetta murder.

Liquor dealer Anthony Pergino was shot by former partner Angus Sangunio over a business disagreement on August 29.

Alfio Alicata was found in a ditch strangled and shot on Fourteen Mile Road near Schoenherr Road in Macomb County. Police believed Alicata was trying to cut in on former LaMare territory, putting him in conflict with both the Eastside Gang and the Westside Gang.

On September 15, Jaspare Valenti—involved with the alky-cooking racket—was gunned down in Monroe, Michigan. The same night, his partner Tony Gravina was cut down in his grocery store at 11515 Cardoni Avenue.

On September 19, Carmelo Castiglione was gunned down by three gunmen while hiding out in his cousin's home at 13832 Gallagher Avenue. Castiglione didn't go down without a fight. As he fell, he shot and killed former partner Tony Capolo.

———

Several weeks after the Fish Market Murders, Chet LaMare quietly returned to his eight-room house in Wyandotte that functioned as his fortress. Loaded guns were stashed in every room. His house was surrounded by a security fence with German shepherds guarding the grounds, and bars were on the windows. LaMare was virtually a prisoner in his own home.

On Friday, February 6, 1931—six months after the Fish Market Murders—Big Chet LaMare and his bodyguard Joe Girardi sat drinking coffee in his kitchen when Chet asked his wife, Anna, to take Girardi home at about 9:30 p.m. When Anna returned, she found her husband's body on the kitchen floor in a pool of blood. She called the police just after midnight and screeched at them when they arrived on the scene, "Go into the kitchen. Look what they've done to my husband."

It became apparent that someone LaMare trusted shot him at close range behind the right ear and through the neck. When questioned by police, Anna said she was out of the house for less than an hour, returning to find her husband dead on the kitchen floor. Forensic investigators could tell from rigor mortis that LaMare had been dead for a minimum of two hours. The clotted blood on LaMare's neck also indicated he was shot well over an hour before Anna LaMare called police.

Confronted with the evidence, Anna changed her story, saying she was out of the house for several hours. When asked what she was doing from about 9:30 p.m. until just after midnight, she fumbled for an answer. Anna was arrested on suspicion of being an accessory to murder but was released on bail to arrange and attend the funeral of her husband. In the meantime, fingerprint experts found Joe Amico and Elmer Macklin's fingerprints on dishes in the LaMare sink. Both men were trusted Westside gangsters who had fled town on a southbound Michigan Central train for parts unknown.

That Sunday through Monday, a steady stream of family, friends, business associates, and interested onlookers passed through the LaMare home to view the body at 15505 Grandville Avenue in Wyandotte. The Westside crime lord was laid out in a $5,000 silver-trimmed casket and buried on Tuesday, February 10, 1931, at Mt. Olivet Cemetery. There were as many uniformed and plainclothes police at the funeral as mourners, but no underworld figures were known to attend.

Most gangland widows were left penniless when their husbands were murdered, but not Big Chet's wife Anna. He left her $500,000 in real estate and told her about his other holdings before he was killed. His widow had been amply provided for.

Over a year after LaMare's murder on April 27, 1932, Amico and Macklin were captured and placed on trial. Defense lawyers convinced Recorders Court Judge John P. Scallen to declare a mistrial because of a prejudicial question asked of witnesses by the prosecution. Five weeks later, on June 9, 1932, Judge Henry S. Sweeny ordered a directed not-guilty verdict because—in his opinion—he did not believe sufficient evidence existed for a successful prosecution. Much to the chagrin of prosecutors, the defendants walked away free.

The murder of Chet LaMare effectively ended the seven-month Crosstown Mob War. The Eastside Mafia emerged stronger and more unified when Joseph Zerilli, William Tocco, Angelo Meli, Peter Licavoli, and John Priziola came out on top. They christened their reconstituted Mafia organization the Detroit Partnership and signed on with the newly formed national crime syndicate La Cosa Nostra headquartered in New York City.

The Purple Gang remained relatively unscathed from the Italian gang war but seemed bent on self-destruction. It was clear the tremors in Detroit's underworld would take their toll on the Purples' organization unless Abe Burnstein could exercise his waning diplomatic skills. His brothers Joe and Isadore had already left town and relocated in California. Now, Ray Burnstein played a larger role in the gang's management and decision making. Seven months later, all hell would break loose.

—14—

The Political Winds Shift

ON AUGUST 9, 1929, Recorder's Court Municipal Judge Charles Bowles announced his plan to resign from the bench and run for mayor against former two-time mayor John W. Smith. Bowles had run twice for the office and lost, but the Republicans felt he could beat Smith this time. Bowles issued a brief statement to the press: "By becoming a candidate for mayor, I am convinced I can serve the city better in that capacity." Judge Bowles was openly supported by the Ku Klux Klan. Conspicuously missing from his announcement was any mention of the platform he would run on. Prior to throwing his hat into the ring, Bowles was best known as the presiding judge for the Cleaners and Dyers War trial where the Purple Gang was first acknowledged publicly. The defendants were acquitted of extortion and racketeering charges despite long rap sheets for other offenses. Bowles's tenure as a municipal judge was unremarkable.

Bowles defeated his Catholic Democratic opponent Smith after two previous attempts and was elected Detroit's fifty-eighth mayor. Even before the Bowles administration was sworn into office, financial trouble loomed on the horizon. With the Wall Street stock market crash of October 1929, the Great Depression tightened its grip on Detroit. To compound matters, Bowles inherited the greatest deficit in the city's history. The attempted assassination of Police Inspector Henry J. Garvin—allegedly by gangsters—and the wounding of Lois Bartlett on her way to school instigated the public outcry for an investigation of police corruption. His opponents portrayed Bowles as tolerant of lawlessness which angered many citizens.

Detroit was the fourth-largest city in the United States after New York, Chicago, and San Francisco. There was no shortage of unsolved civic problems. Rampant unemployment was the growing menace everyone feared the most. Rather than starve, many people resorted to petty street crime and violence. Times were tough and people were desperate. The carnage on Detroit streets was upsetting to the public, and something had to be done about it.

The expectation of Bowles's supporters was high. Fifteen hundred of Detroit's "finest" people attended the inaugural celebration at the Masonic Temple. Even as a gang war raged and the murder rate rose, Bowles boldly claimed in his inaugural address that his administration would clean up Detroit of its underworld influence in the police department and city hall.

"The first obligation of public officers of this community," Bowles said, "is to disarm the gunmen. The gunman, the kidnapper, and every brand of criminal must be brought to understand that the city of Detroit is an unsafe place for their operations." The crowd applauded wildly.

"It is unfortunate, but nevertheless an admitted fact, that blind pigs (low-end speakeasies without gambling or entertainment) have flourished and multiplied within the city—until today—they are found in every locality. I believe, however, that the most vicious and most dangerous of these are the ones located within close proximity of our schools." This was the mayor's subtle acknowledgement of the Lois Bartlett shooting.

Mayor Bowles caught political observers by surprise when he announced that Harold H. Emmons, a well-known and respected businessman without prior police experience, was chosen as the new police commissioner. Rather than promote someone from within the department, Bowles felt he needed to appoint someone from the outside with successful management experience to restore order and discipline among the ranks. After all, a new broom sweeps clean.

Emmons held a law degree from the University of Michigan and was a veteran of World War I. He was awarded the Distinguished Service Medal by the Secretary of War—the first naval officer so honored. During the war, he was appointed chief of the Aircraft Production Board in charge of twenty-three plants around the country. His department delivered thirty-two thousand Liberty engines to the government. Here was a man who knew how to manage a large organization and get things done.

Emmons was also active in Detroit's social scene. He spent the past two and a half years as the president of the Detroit Board of Commerce and was a well-known member of the Detroit Athletic Club, the Detroit Golf Club, the Detroit Boat Club, the Bloomfield Hills Country Club, the Lawyer's Club, the Detroit Bar Association, the American Legion, and the Society of Automotive Engineers.

In Emmons's first statement to the press, he promised "a nice, clean police administration." When questioned about the "tangled and odoriferous mass of charges, innu-endos, and investigations growing out of the Garvin case," he answered prudently, "I will comment on the case after I study and know more about it."

———

Mayor Bowles stirred a hornet's nest in February when he announced his 1930 budget plans. Huge amounts were to be cut from the board of education, the school construc-tion fund, the public assistance program, the public health system, and the library budget. Bowles also announced a hike in street car fares which everyone who took the trolley would feel immediately. Bowles vowed he would do every-thing in his power not to borrow money or raise taxes. His fiscal philosophy was "pay as we go."

Even with the deep budget cuts, the property tax levy was calculated to rise from twenty-three dollars to twenty-seven dollars per thousand dollars—the highest rate in the city's history. The actual amount turned out to be twenty-four dollars. Still, taxes are taxes and everyone grumbled. His "no new taxes" promise was just the first of the mayor's ten campaign promises he was unable to keep.

The mayor did support the purchase of twenty-seven new police cruisers with radio equipment to help police in their fight against crime. Now, police patrols could coordi-nate their efforts not having to find a phone booth and make a call to the station. Few citizens would complain about that expenditure. This was tangible proof the mayor meant business when he portrayed himself as a crime fighter.

The press was focused on the gang war and the shakeup in the police department. Reporters pressed the mayor's office for answers. Rather than address their questions in a forthright manner, Bowles was annoyed and attacked the press. He complained of being the victim of a media witch hunt. Detroit's citizens were being gunned down in the streets with alarming regularity, but Bowles focused on the bad press he was getting. The mayor issued a news blackout for his staff to refuse all interviews. The public interpreted this to mean the mayor had something to hide. Soon, Bowles was portrayed in the newspapers as a tool for the underworld. Alienating the press was not a winning strategy for Bowles and contributed to a recall campaign against him.

———

In the spring and summer of 1930, speakeasies and gambling joints downtown were on the increase as was violent street crime. On July 3 at 6:30 p.m., three men were shot while sitting in a parked car across the street from the LaSalle Hotel. Two banished Chicago hoods—William Cannon and George Collins—were shot dead. A third man cowering in the back seat survived three slugs fired at him. His name was Mike Stitzel—a small-time Detroit hood. With not so gentle persuasion, Detroit police detectives leaned hard on Stitzel. He admitted acting as a finger man (spotter) for the Chicago interlopers. Stitzel said the dead men carried gold badges with "Special Police" inscribed on them. The out-of-town pair used their phony badges to shakedown people and extort money from Italian speakeasies and disorderly houses (brothels). Stitzel said he steered Cannon and Collins away from Purple Gang–protected establishments.

The Chicago pair had an end game. They wanted to establish themselves in the narcotics trade. Stitzel said they were waiting outside the hotel to make a drug deal. Then a dark man walked up to the car with his head tipped so his hat shielded his face. He opened fire on them and ran off into the alley. Stitzel couldn't or wouldn't identify the man, but swift police work identified the killer as Leonardo "Black Leo" Cellura. A fugitive for six years, Cellura finally appeared one day with his lawyer at police headquarters. Cellura was charged with the Cannon and Collins murders and pled not guilty by reason of self-defense. His first trial ended in a mistrial, but the second trial convicted him of murder in the first degree resulting in a life sentence.

———

Gangland murders were so rampant in 1930 that Detroit reporters dubbed them the "Bloody Thirties." In July alone, fourteen men were slain—all but three were involved in the rackets. Since 1928, Gerald Emmett Buckley had been a nightly radio broadcast commentator on WMBC from six until seven with a popular program entitled the *Buckley Hour*. He helped instigate a special election to recall Mayor Bowles. Buckley was an outspoken political commentator and Bowles's primary media tormentor. The murders of Cannon and Collins just nineteen days before the recall special election of Mayor Bowles reverberated nightly over the radio airwaves. Buckley railed against the rise in crime in downtown Detroit since Bowles took office and criticized his administration, which by Buckley's estimation was the most corrupt in the city's long history.

Buckley was born into a well-to-do family in the Detroit Irish neighborhood of Corktown. He was the product of Catholic parochial schools and earned his law degree at Detroit College of Law. Buckley began his crusade against the underworld as an investigator for the Ford Motor Company (FoMoCo). Outraged by the corruption he witnessed at FoMoCo, Buckley quit and became a staff reporter at WMBC radio broadcasting from the LaSalle Hotel on Woodward Avenue and Adelaide Street. Before long, he became an on-air radio personality.

The *Buckley Hour* was Detroit's most popular radio show. Buckley championed humanitarian causes and the plight of the unemployed who he called the "common herd." He was heralded by the press the "friend of the poor." Nightly, he railed against political corruption and organized crime influence openly accusing the Bowles administration of collusion with local mobsters.

While Bowles was out of town at the Kentucky Derby wagering on the ponies, his new police commissioner at the prompting of the press took the initiative and launched a series of coordinated raids on Detroit racetrack handbook operations. To the public, Emmons appeared the real crime fighter in the Bowles administration. Special police squad task force units cracked down on underworld gambling establishments downtown on May 17. Within fifteen hours, between 9:00 a.m. and midnight, Emmons's raiders arrested thirty-four men and nine women as "frequenters" of gambling and blind pig establishments. Gambling equipment and stores of whiskey and beer were destroyed, and a large amount of money was confiscated.

When the mayor returned to Detroit from the Derby, he fired his highly regarded police commissioner for acting in his absence. As a direct result, Gerald Buckley redoubled his nightly tirades against government graft and corruption in the Bowles administration. Bowles's collusion with local underworld figures brought Buckley into direct conflict with some of Detroit's most powerful and dangerous gangsters. After advocating for the recall campaign of Mayor Bowles, Buckley began receiving daily death threats. "If the recall vote is successful, you're a dead man," he was told.

Buckley made a charge on his radio program that gambling concerns in the city contributed $60,000 to $80,000 to the Bowles campaign to defeat John W. Smith, the democratic candidate, preventing Smith from winning a third term. Buckley reported that police crime statistics proved crime had doubled since Bowles took office five months before.

Persons from all walks of life were signing recall petitions to oust Bowles. Recall committee chairman Walter B. Cary announced on June 16 that 111,270 recall petition signatures were collected but only 90,000 signatures were necessary to call a special election. All the signatures were certified Detroit residents but not necessarily registered voters. Mayor Bowles's lawyers tried to stop the recall election in the Wayne County Circuit Court but failed. Wayne County Judge Arthur Webster held that the courts did not have the right to interfere with the will of the people. "The recall is a political matter," Judge Webster ruled. The city council provided $65,000 for the recall election and set the date for July 22.

The ten reasons for the recall were printed on the ballot:

1. Mayor Bowles tolerated lawlessness by law enforcement agencies.

2. He delegated lawyer Frank Dohany to disavow claims against the street railway's claims department.

3. Gave John Gillespie, a professional lobbyist and

bondsman, control of Detroit's public works program to make deals with contractors who made him wealthy.

4. Gave John Gillespie official direction of waste management despite his private monopoly of the trash collection business.

5. Destroyed efficient public service through dismissal of faithful employees.

6. Attempted to increase street car fares and discharged Commissioner James Couzens.

7. Made fifteen pledges before the election but kept none.

8. Directed his staff to keep public records secret.

9. Seeks to create a political machine of street railway workers and other city employees by manipulation of patronage and public funds.

10. Hindered Police Commissioner Harold H. Emmons in his enforcement of the law and discharged him for enforcing the law while the mayor was out of town.

Fighting for his political life, Mayor Bowles spoke before a crowd of three hundred people at the Cosmic Men's Club sponsored by the Fort Street Congregational Church. Bowles declared, "I'm not worried by the recall campaign. What I regret most is the bad advertising it gives the city all over the rest of the country.

"This recall thing is a racket like many other rackets," the mayor explained. "If you pay the price, you may hire someone (Gerald Buckley) to talk for you on the radio. If you don't pay the price, you are abused.

"Petitioners are paid so much apiece for signatures, but I'm not worried, I know how many signatures they have. Political racketeers and disgruntled losers are behind it, aided and abetted by the stories in the newspapers. It's too bad for the city.

"Concerning my firing of Harold Emmons, he was an absolute failure as police commissioner. Emmons is the most incompetent city official I have ever seen, and the charge that I tied his hands and kept these gambling joints open is slander. As far as the rising murder rate in the city, it's just as well to permit these gangsters to shoot each other to death."

In a radio response to Mayor Bowles's callous remark about the raging gang war on the city's streets, recall chairman Walter B. Cary asked listeners, "What is to prevent innocent bystanders from being shot? Both Mayor Bowles and his new police commissioner Thomas C. Wilcox are violating their oaths by tolerating these gangster slayings. There have been ten gangster killings in the last eleven days. The shooting of Inspector Garvin and eleven-year-old Lois Bartlett was an overshadowing reason for the recall of Mayor Bowles. Detroiters want their streets and homes safe."

The Cannon and Collins shooting in early July across the street from the LaSalle Hotel where his WMBC studio was located left a stark impression on Gerald Buckley. The timing of the murders couldn't have been worse for Mayor Bowles. Buckley hammered away on Bowles nightly as the date of the recall election neared. Buckley was warned again by an anonymous source that if the recall was successful, he would be killed. The threat did nothing to silence the crime crusader. Buckley continued his nightly attacks on Bowles.

But the mayor had his supporters too. Protestant Reverend William C. S. Pellows—in his radio broadcast sermon on Sunday, May 25—criticized the *Detroit News* for its "brainless journalistic policy of constant attacks since the first moments of Mayor Bowles's administration. To pillory a man day after day, to hound him one way or another, trying to throw him off poise is little more the persecution.

"Then there is the recall .... One would think that the mayor had put millions of the people's money into his own bank account, or had shot somebody, or had spit on the flag, or had lapsed into moral turpitude. I personally believe in the integrity and sincerity of the mayor. To plunge this city into a whirlpool of bitter personal feuds would be a catastrophe, not to mention the costly special election."

Early morning July 23, Buckley left election headquarters at city hall and walked to the WMBC studios to file his election report at 12:15 a.m. Mayor Charles Bowles was recalled by a decisive majority. The balloting in the special election was the heaviest in the city's history. Mayor Bowles was beaten by 30,956 votes. John Gillespie, commissioner of public works and manager of the Bowles campaign, conceded defeat at 10:25 p.m. Bowles was the only mayor of a large American city ever recalled. The defeat was a total repudiation of Bowles and his administration.

While at the radio studio, Buckley got a call from an unidentified woman who agreed to meet him in the lobby of the LaSalle. At about 1:20 a.m., Buckley's wife, Jeanette, answered their home phone thinking it was her husband.

"Your husband won't be coming home tonight," a female voice said before hanging up.

After Buckley finished his special recall election radio report, he went down to the lobby, sat in an easy chair, and began reading the newspaper while he waited. That was at 1:30 a.m. Next to him sat motion picture exhibitor Jack Klein—a known Purple Gang drug dealer. At about 1:45 a.m., Angelo Livecchi—LaSalle resident—stood by the Woodward Avenue entrance as a lookout and finger man. He pointed Buckley out to three gunmen who rushed into the lobby and opened fire, pumping eleven slugs into the radio crusader. Jack Klein hit the floor and took cover. A wheelman was waiting in a small gray sedan outside the Adelaide Street entrance. The triggermen made a hasty retreat to the waiting getaway car.

A second car driven by a woman a witness described as a "big blonde" skidded sideways, blocking Woodward Avenue and Adelaide Street giving the getaway car a clean escape. She ran into a theater for cover. Several minutes later she returned for her car with detectives waiting for her. The driver was Lucille Love, but detectives recognized her as the girlfriend of local Mafioso Angelo Livecchi, who coincidently lived at the LaSalle.

Miss Love said she was approaching the hotel to return her boyfriend Angelo's car, so he could take her home when she heard gunshots. Love said she panicked, slamming on the car's brakes skidding sideways in the middle of the street before stopping. Love claimed she ran into a nearby theater lobby across the street for cover because she was scared to death by all the people being killed on Detroit streets lately. Police released Love on her own recognizance. Miss Love was called to testify at the trial but was never arrested or directly implicated in the Buckley murder plot.

WMBC radio engineer W. S. Martin reported to police that he watched from a window on the eleventh floor of the north side of the hotel as the killers jumped into their waiting car and fled. Martin identified the trio as Joe Bommarito, Angelo Livecchi, and Ted Pizzino. Soon after speaking to the police, Martin wisely quit his job and left Detroit. The Wayne County prosecutor's staff traced him to Jackson and then Grand Rapids. After that, the trail went cold.

———•———

The first police theory put forward held that Buckley was hit as revenge for the successful recall victory against Bowles. Soon, rumors were floated to the press that Gerald Buckley was not the crime crusader for the "common herd" he purported to be on the radio. Bowles appointee, Police Commissioner Thomas C. Wilcox, took no time to allege that Buckley was a known womanizer, nightclub patron, extortionist, and racketeer. Soon, it was tossed around that Buckley double-crossed the Eastside River Gang to the tune of $40,000 in a deal that fell through. Another rumor held that the underworld paid off Buckley to keep him from dropping their names and exposing their criminal enterprises. Sickened by these charges, Gerald Buckley's brother Paul countered that his brother's estate amounted to only $150 in cash.

The slanderous rumors only solidified the high regard in which Buckley was held by the public. Friends of Buckley quickly came to his defense and denied the false claims, dismissing them as a desperate attempt to discredit the popular, slain crusader who devoted his life to public service and projects for the relief of men and women out of work and in want. Buckley was a true friend of the poor and downtrodden, they insisted.

———

Gerald Buckley's body was laid out for public viewing in his home at 4031 Pasadena Avenue from Thursday afternoon until Saturday morning. It was estimated that thirty thousand mourners filed four abreast night and day through the Buckley home. Most people only knew him as a voice on the radio championing their causes and ideals. Private funeral services were held at his home at 8:30 a.m. on Sunday. A requiem mass was conducted by Father Francis F. Van Antwerp at St. Gregory's Catholic Church. Estimates of fifty to one hundred thousand mourners lined the streets leading to Mt. Olivet Cemetery, making this the largest funeral Detroit had ever seen. As the coffin was lowered into the grave on a sweltering gray afternoon, "Taps" was played as men and women wept.

The following day, the *Detroit Free Press* ran a letter to the editor from Mrs. Thelma Young that summed up the feelings of many Detroit residents:

"I am one of thousands utterly shocked and overcome with horror on hearing the most cruel and cowardly murder of our beloved radio man Jerry Buckley. He had endeared himself to the hearts of the downtrodden masses and the working people whose loyal and true friends Mr. Buckley ever was. The public is deeply grieved and bitter tears were shed.

"It is an overwhelming blot of shame on the city of Detroit that things are in such rotten condition that it is possible for such a thing to happen. The whole city should hang its head before the eyes of God and man until Jerry Buckley's murder has been avenged. Some vipers are trying to besmirch his good name with their foul lies. May God's curse rest on all of them."

———

Investigators quickly discovered that three Eastside mob gunmen—Theodore Pizzino, Angelo Livecchi, and Leonard "Black Leo" Cellura—shared a room at the LaSalle as their headquarters. But Cellura was still at large because of the Cannon and Collins murders earlier in July. He was out of the picture.

Angelo Livecchi was identified as being in the lobby presumably waiting for his girlfriend, Lucille Love, to pick him up. He ran for cover in the elevator when the shooting began. Police found Livecchi hiding in his hotel room and arrested him. Ted Pizzino left town after the shooting and thereby drew suspicion upon himself. He turned up in New York City. After fighting extradition for four months, Pizzino was returned in leg irons and under armed guard to Detroit from Manhattan. More than one hundred detectives and two machine gun squads protected their prisoner on his train journey to Detroit. A third man—Joseph Bommarito, identified as one of the shooters—was the first of the suspected killers to be indicted. Bommarito was a known Mafia lieutenant with a long rap sheet.

Indictments were brought by a twenty-one person grand jury a full year after the Buckley murder. Angelo Livecchi, Ted Pizzino, and Joe Bommarito were finally brought to trial. After six weeks of tedious testimony, the case was turned over to a jury on April 20, 1931. Judge Edward J. Jefferies instructed the jury of eight men and four women that they could either find the defendants guilty of murder in the first degree or acquit them. After thirty-five hours of jury deliberations, all three defendants were acquitted of Gerald Buckley's murder. Outside the courtroom after the trial, the jury foreman told the press that it took three jury ballots to acquit Joe Bommarito, two for Angelo Livecchi, and thirteen for Ted Pizzino.

The public lost even more confidence in the criminal justice system's ability to make a conviction stick against Detroit's powerful underworld. But one positive result of the murder trial was there were increased police raids on nightclubs, bookie joints, and brothels. Another positive outcome was public opinion finally turned against organized crime. Detroit was no longer the wide-open town it was before Buckley's murder. Outraged citizens were ready to stand up and testify in court against the underworld.

—15—

The Collingwood Manor Massacre

September 16, 1931

AL CAPONE INHERITED THE Chicago mob from Johnny Torrio in 1925 after Torrio narrowly escaped death from a brutal assassination attempt. One of Capone's first acts was to consolidate his power and define his territory. His men ran ambitious, independent operators out of town. Three of those men—Izzy Sutker, Joe Leibovitz, and Hymie Paul—pulled up stakes in Chicago and traveled to Detroit to try their hand at smuggling Canadian liquor and beer which was a burgeoning business with unlimited growth potential.

The three men associated themselves with a gang named the Third Avenue Terrors, who were headquartered at the Third Avenue Tavern a couple of blocks from the waterfront. The Terrors were foot soldiers affiliated with the Purple Gang who specialized in hijacking shipments from would-be competitors. They also operated several horseracing betting parlors. They were known and feared for their ruthless violence. As an incentive, the Purple Gang allowed the Terrors to operate in a small area of the city in return for weekly kickbacks from their earnings.

When Capone cut a lucrative deal with the Purple Gang to supply his organization with all the liquor they could smuggle, Sutker, Leibovitz, and Paul recognized an opportunity and began buying speedboats at bargain prices from Detroit police auctions that sold assets confiscated in alcohol raids. As their fleet grew, so did their dominance smuggling on the waterfront. The splinter group quickly earned the gang name the Little Jewish Navy.

Not satisfied with being mere foot soldiers for the Purples and taking their share of bootlegging profits, the gang began shaking down mob-protected businesses around the city to raise capital. The Little Jewish Navy showed no respect for the established territories of other gangs. When some of their junior members were caught red-handed shaking down an Italian-owned speakeasy, the truth was beaten out of them until they ratted out gang leaders Sutker, Leibowitz, and Paul. Then, the battered and bruised stool pigeons disappeared from Detroit never to be seen again.

The Little Jewish Navy wanted to establish themselves as major players in Detroit's underworld, so Izzy Sutker and Solomon Levine went into a bookie joint partnership tied to the Purple Gang's subscription wire service. Levine had grown up on the Lower Eastside with Joe and Ray Burnstein and regarded them as personal friends. Rather than drop out of public school in the eighth grade like many kids from their Paradise Valley neighborhood, Sol graduated from high school and went on to business college earning an accounting degree.

After keeping the books for his father's scrap metal

business for several years, Sol was drawn to the rackets by the easy money and the fast life. Levine began his underworld career by bootlegging and hijacking liquor shipments from Canada; then, he became a liquor cutter and eventually opened a bookie joint working out of a Selden Avenue storefront. Sol was known to finance some of the Little Jewish Navy's operations and was responsible for introducing the three transplanted Chicago gangsters to the Burnstein brothers.

Izzy Sutker borrowed $13,000 worth of bootleg liquor on credit from Ray Burnstein, which Sutker's people cut and began wholesaling around town undercutting prices set by the Purples. Then, Solomon and Sutker's sport's book took on heavy losses one week which they were hard-pressed to pay. Rather than pay Ray Burnstein back his $13,000, Levine and Sutker chose to pay off their handbook losses. Now they were desperate for money. Sutker needed and asked for two more weeks to earn enough money from an upcoming American Legion convention to pay Burnstein back. Prior to their handbook losses, Sutker, Leibowitz, and Paul wanted to negotiate a bigger piece of the liquor business by becoming the Purple Gang's sole suppliers.

Ray Burnstein was suspicious of Sutker and his partners. After talking it over with his brother Abe, he was prepared to offer a concession to the group as a way to draw the three schemers together. To avoid further trouble down the road, Ray Burnstein wanted these interlopers eliminated before they grew strong enough to muscle in on the rest of the Purple's rackets.

Burnstein ran into Sol Levine innocently enough outside Levinson's Restaurant on Woodward Avenue in the heart of Purple Gang territory. Burnstein casually chatted with

Levine, mentioning that he and his brothers wanted to phase out of the bootlegging business and go legit. They were weary of the violence and police harassment of the illegal liquor business. The cover story was they had decided to offer Sutker, Leibowitz, and Paul what they wanted. Burnstein sweetened the deal by offering them the counterfeit whiskey label printing business. Ray Burnstein said he would call Levine to arrange a meeting to discuss the prospect with the three men. Sol Levine risked straining his friendship with Burnstein by asking for more time to pay off Sutker's debt until after the Legionnaires convention in two weeks. Burnstein agreed to meet with the Little Jewish Navy leadership to work out the details of the loan.

The following day at 2:00 p.m., Burnstein called and arranged to meet with Levine and the others at the Collingwood Manor Apartments in apartment 211 at 3:00 p.m. Sutker, Leibovitz, and Paul were ambitious to advance in Detroit's underworld and anxious to take the meeting. They were getting the green light to be bosses in their own right. Sol Levine agreed to pick up the three men and meet Burnstein within the hour.

Sutker let Levine drive to the Collingwood Manor in Sutker's new DeSoto sedan. Levine parked out front. As a show of good faith, the four men were unarmed. They entered the lobby and gave it the once-over. Levine led them to the stairwell. On the second floor, Levine knocked on the door of apartment 211. Burnstein opened it smiling, inviting the men into the apartment to have a seat. The four men looked around and saw paint tarps in the kitchen spread on the countertop and the floor. A bucket of paint was under the sink. "The landlord is painting the kitchen," Ray Burnstein said.

The Purple Gang chieftain brought three Purple Gang lieutenants—Harry Keywell, Irving Milberg, and Harry Fleisher—to make sure there were no misunderstandings. The Purples stood up and shook hands with the Little Jewish Navy leaders. The four men sat on the couch while the three Purples brought kitchen chairs into the living room to sit on. Ray Burnstein stood smoking a cigarette.

After exchanging some small talk, Ray Burnstein got down to business. He wanted the $13,000 Sutker owed him. Burnstein told Sutker that he and his brothers were ready to take a step back from the day-to-day liquor business. The Jewish Navy could act as their sole liquor agents, but first the loan came due. Ray wanted his money.

Sutker said he and his boys were confident they could raise the money during the American Legion Convention at the end of the month. Burnstein agreed but reminded Sutker he would owe an additional week of interest. Hymie Paul asked what the exact figure would be; Ray didn't know off the top of his head. Irving Milberg told Burnstein to go down to the corner drugstore and call Scotty—the gang's accountant—from a phone booth there. The small-time hoods knew the interest on the loan would eat up their convention profits, but they had no choice but agree. This was an all-or-nothing opportunity and the potential profits would be huge. They patiently waited.

The seven men left behind in the apartment began some small talk to ease the awkward silence and kill some time while Ray Burnstein called Scotty and walked back from the drugstore. Suddenly, a car horn blared from the alley, and its driver revved its engine until the car backfired. On cue, the Purple Gang members stood up and unloaded their .38-caliber Colt revolvers into the bodies of Sutker, Leibovitz, and Paul leaving Sol Levine in wide-eyed terror at the unforeseen carnage. Fleisher wanted to murder Levine too—which would have been the smart thing to do—but Milberg and Keywell stopped him. Burnstein had given specific orders that his school pal Solly be spared. The three assassins dropped their guns in a bucket of green paint under the sink.

"Thank Ray for your life, Solly," Fleisher said. "Now, let's get out of here."

The four men rushed out of the apartment, descended the stairwell, and left by the alley door. Ray Burnstein was waiting for them behind the wheel of his black Chrysler sedan. The assassins jumped into the car and sped down the alley almost hitting a truck on the cross street. Burnstein dropped Milberg and Fleisher off a few blocks away and drove on with Keywell and Levine for a few more blocks. Burnstein and Keywell dropped Levine off by himself, giving him cab fare to his Selden Avenue sports book.

"Don't forget, I'm your pal, Solly," Burnstein said.

"Sure, I know that, Ray," Levine said, still in shock from what he witnessed.

"We'll send a car over to pick you up later."

"Sure, sure," Levine said as Burnstein and Keywell sped away.

Minutes later, Frank Holt—Collingwood Manor building supervisor—banged on the door of apartment 211. When nobody answered, he used his passkey. Something was blocking the door. Holt forced the door open enough to see the gruesome sight of three men on the floor with blood pools oozing onto the floor boards. Holt quickly pulled the door shut and phoned the police from his apartment. A large contingent of detectives showed up within minutes.

Some of them surveyed the crime scene while others sought witnesses.

Police found several witnesses who saw the men leave through the alley. Harry McDonald managed the apartment building across the alley from the Collingwood Manor. "There was a man behind the wheel of a black sedan parked in the alley," McDonald said. "He was leaning on the horn and gunning his engine. I heard ten or twelve shots which I thought at first was the engine backfiring. I was about to shout from my kitchen window for him to knock it off when four well-dressed men ran out of the building, jumped into the car, and sped away. It wasn't until the police arrived some time later that I found out three men were murdered over there."

Mrs. Morris Niss lived on the ground floor beneath the murder apartment. She told reporters, "I heard shots and bodies falling on the floor. I ran into the hallway with my crying baby, and a man brushed quickly past me. I didn't get a good look at him as his hat hid his face. He took two steps at a time down the stairs to the alley. Then, I heard a car roar away."

Another witness was a teenage boy waiting in the alley to walk his younger brother home from school. Detectives talked to him but sent him and his brother home before reporters could question him.

The Purples made themselves scarce on Detroit streets, conspicuous by their absence. Once Levine made it back to his betting parlor, he nervously mentioned to some cohorts that he narrowly escaped with his life, but Sutker, Leibowitz, and Paul weren't so lucky. One of the people Levine told feared reprisals and tipped off police.

It didn't take long for police investigators to arrive and

arrest Levine at this betting parlor. When interrogated, he concocted a story about being kidnapped by unknown gangsters and somehow managed to escape with his life. Unconvinced, Detroit police detectives impressed upon Levine what he already feared—he was a dead man if he didn't come clean and start cooperating with them. Realizing his chances of survival without police protection were slim and none, Levine became a stool pigeon and turned state's evidence.

Levine told investigators he brought three of his associates to the Collingwood for a meeting with some Purple Gang members to smooth over some misunderstandings between them. Levine said he was duped into bringing the men to the Collingwood Manor and had no idea he was leading them into a trap. Levine put the finger on Irving Milberg for shooting Hymie Paul, Harry Keywell for shooting Izzy Sutker, and Harry Fleisher for shooting Joe Leibowitz. Ray Burnstein set the trap and was the wheelman for the triple murder.

At Levine's arraignment, Judge Thomas M. Cotter set bail for $500,000—the highest bond ever set for a material witness in the state of Michigan. Levine shrugged his shoulders, saying, "I wouldn't furnish bond if it was five dollars, Your Honor. I'm safer in jail than free on the street."

The Wayne County prosecutor requested a team of eight police bodyguards to protect their star witness night and day, seven days a week. Throughout the investigation and trial, Solomon Levine was cloistered in a jail cell deep in the bowels of 1300 Beaubien—Detroit Police Headquarters. Even the brash Purple Gang wouldn't attempt to hit Levine there.

The police fanned out to locate the conspirators but came up empty until Chief of Detectives James McCarthy received an anonymous phone tip. In a muffled voice, the caller said, "Two of the men you want for the Collingwood murders are at 2649 Calvert Street. You better hurry because within an hour, they'll be out of town." Then, the line went dead. McCarthy thought the caller sounded Italian.

A heavily-armed police team from the Canfield precinct surrounded the house of Purple Gang consultant Charles Auerback. The evening raid found Ray Burnstein and Harry Keywell in their pajamas. Both men were arrested, handcuffed, and taken to jail. A search of Auerback's house produced a cache of weapons, ammunition, and tear gas shells. Auerback was also arrested for harboring fugitives from the law. In addition, police confiscated $9,025 in crisp fifty and one-hundred-dollar bills found in Elise Carroll's purse. Carroll was a vaudeville entertainer and Keywell's girlfriend. Investigators believed the money was from the robbery of Ben Aronoff in Toledo, Ohio. His betting parlor was taken for approximately $10,000 in new fifty and one-hundred-dollar bills by thugs using a submachine gun in the heist. The next morning, gunman Irving Milberg was arrested in his home while packing to leave town.

Only Harry Fleisher remained at large. He was the only one of the four suspects with the good sense to leave town quickly after the murders. Fleisher went directly to his rented flat to change out of his suit into some street clothes and grab his bugout bag. Fleisher gave his wife, Hattie, a cash-filled envelope before she tearfully embraced him and said good-bye, not knowing if she would ever see him alive again. Hattie watched Harry speed away, disappearing around a street corner in a Ford coupe she didn't recognize.

During the 1920s and 1930s, the world was considerably less documented, and law enforcement cooperation among different agencies was inefficient at best. There were no national fingerprint databases, networked computers, DNA identification, or even Social Security numbers to assist law enforcement. It was still possible for a wanted man to simply disappear, and that's what Fleisher did until he turned himself in on June 9, 1932—nine months after the Collingwood Massacre.

At a hastily arranged noon press conference two days after the massacre, Bert C. Brown—chief of the United States Secret Service in Detroit—reported, "Three of the four Purple Gangsters suspected in the murders at the Collingwood Apartments are in police custody, while federal authorities are in hot pursuit of Harry Fleisher, who is believed to be armed and dangerous. We ask for the public's help in bringing this fugitive to justice. Anyone with information about Mr. Fleisher should contact the offices of the United States Secret Service downtown. I'll take your questions now."

"Chief Brown, can you tell us anything about the men who were killed?" asked a *Detroit Free Press* reporter.

"The murder victims were not exactly Purple Gang members but affiliated with them. The gang is known as the Little Jewish Navy. Apparently, the victims were bootleggers, hijackers, and kidnappers, but we're still investigating their links to the Purples."

A *Detroit News* reporter asked, "Is there any indication that Detroit is headed for another gang war?"

"That's tough to say until we get more information," Chief Brown said. "Events like this often signal a reorganization of the power structure within a gang. We haven't seen anything like this in Detroit since the Milaflores Massacre two years ago. Detectives believe this bloodbath was meant to send a message. It doesn't appear to be a vendetta murder as far as we know at this time."

"Are you seeking other suspects?" a reporter inquired.

"We've arrested known Purple Gang enforcers Ed Fletcher and Abe Axler as suspects but had to release them for lack of evidence."

The Fletcher and Axler arrests were meant to send a message to the rest of the Purples that their days dominating Detroit's underworld were numbered. The message wasn't lost on the Mafia gangs in the Detroit area either. The Eastside River Gang worked with Purple Gang members on projects of mutual interest throughout the 1920s, but as circumstances unfolded in the 1930s, Anthony "Uno" Zerilli and William "Black Bill" Tocco began plotting their takeover of Detroit's underworld.

—16—

The Collingwood Trial

AT THE OPENING DAY of the Collingwood Manor murder trial in Detroit Recorder's Court on November 2, 1931, over one hundred heavily armed policemen guarded the courthouse. Solomon Levine was surrounded by twelve, burly homicide detectives as he was led into the courtroom. For this first day of the trial, eight hundred people showed up vying for a place in the spectator galley—limited to five hundred by order of the fire marshal. Beginning at 8:00 a.m., spectators in groups of three were allowed into the courtroom only after being frisked for weapons. A police matron was on duty to pat down the women and check their purses.

Among those not allowed inside the courthouse was Purple Gang leader Abraham Burnstein—the only Burnstein brother excluded from the opening-day proceedings. Abe had traveled by train from Miami, Florida, to show solidarity with his younger brother Ray. *Detroit Times* staff reporter wrote a portrait of how Abe was attired for his brother's murder trial: "Sleekly dressed in a symphony of

177

green, Abe Burnstein wore a dark green suit, light green dress shirt, a tie to match, and a green silk kerchief peeping from his coat pocket."

The elder Burnstein tried to use his blood relationship to one of the defendants to gain entrance into the courthouse. Unsympathetic, Detective Leo Doyle told him, "Get in line like everyone else, big shot." Perturbed, Abe Burnstein walked to the front steps of the Recorder's Court with his personal security and sought out members of the press who were milling around outside. The *Detroit Times* was the only newspaper admitted in the courtroom, as it was chosen the newspaper of record. The rest of the Detroit press and media was outside scrambling for a story. Taking a page out of Al Capone's book on public relations, Abe directly addressed the news-starved reporters and radio announcers.

"Here we are, hardworking people trying to make a living in Detroit and minding our own business, and they won't leave us alone," Burnstein observed.

"Who won't leave you alone, Abe?" a local reporter asked.

"The Detroit Police, the Wayne County Prosecutor, the Federal Police, that's who. Sure, we used to bootleg and live the good life in the twenties, but since then we've been going straight, trying to scratch out an honest living in these hard times like everyone else in this town. Every time there's a murder or a shootout, the Purple Gang gets blamed in the papers. All I see is 'the Purple Gang this' and 'the Purple gang that' in the headlines. I don't even know what the Purple Gang is. It's bunk! There is no Purple Gang—never was."

"Why do you think security is so tight for this trial?"

"The prosecutor is grandstanding—plain and simple."

"Can you elaborate, Mr. Burnstein?"

"All this is designed to prejudice the case against the defendants. Yes, all this bunk about searching spectators for weapons. Prosecutor Toy wants the public and the jurors to think that our family will try to kill Solly Levine in the courtroom for squealing. It's all bunk. Once Levine is proven to be a liar and his real motives are revealed, Ray and the other men will be set free. I'm convinced of it."

"Can we quote you on that?"

"Every word," Burnstein said as he walked down the remaining steps of the courthouse and entered his Cadillac limo with his associates in tow.

All of Detroit's newspapers began referring to the gang in print as "the so-called" or "the alleged Purple Gang." Abe's foray into public relations may have paid off because the press now cast doubt about the existence of such a gang. For the remainder of the trial, Abe joined his brother Joe and Isadore in the front-row gallery to show family support for Ray.

Of those who made it into the courtroom the first day was high-rolling gambler William "Lefty Clark" Bischoff, who was associated with the Italian mafia. The bookies were already placing bets and setting odds on the case. "Lefty" had a personal stake for being in the courtroom. He was the victim of a classic snatch racket to the tune of $40,000, thought to be tied in with the Purple Gang. Lefty hedged his bets but wanted to see Burnstein, Milberg, and Keywell go down. Though indicted with the rest, Harry Fleisher was still at large.

Security was placed around the gallery to keep an eye on underworld figures scattered throughout the courtroom. Interest ran high in Detroit's black community because of the slaying of seventeen-year-old Arthur Mixon by two recently convicted Purple Gang members—Philip Keywell and Morris Raider. The Mixon supporters came to see Phil's brother Harry on trial.

Few women were present in the courtroom the first day, but that changed as the case stretched on. Young women would miss classes from school or take a day or two off from work to attend the trial and chance sitting next to a real gangster. Mrs. Bertha Milberg sat in the front row of the spectators' gallery. She cut a striking figure in the otherwise dour courtroom. Mrs. Dora Sutker—Izzy's widow—also attended the first day of the trial sitting near the back of the spectators' gallery.

———

Selecting a jury panel for this case had already taken four days. From the moment the jury was sworn in, they were sequestered and virtual prisoners of the state from midafternoon on Friday until Monday morning of the trial. The jurors stayed in a specially constructed dormitory set up on the top floor of the Municipal Court Building to keep intruders out and prevent jury tampering. Three shifts of four policemen and two matrons were charged with the jury's safety. Everyone was on edge and anxious to get the case underway.

Wayne County prosecutors Harry S. Toy and Miles N. Cullehan were prepared and ready, but things were not going well for the defense. Recorder's Court Judge Donald Van Zile wanted court to begin promptly at 10:00 a.m., but lead defense attorney Edward Kennedy Jr. was not present in the courtroom.

"Mr. Baxter," Judge Van Zile asked the defense co-

council, "Do you have any idea what's keeping Mr. Kennedy from being on time this morning?"

"I can't image, Your Honor, but I'm sure Mr. Kennedy will be here shortly," Rodney Baxter replied.

The defendants fidgeted in their barrister chairs at the defense table. Irving Milberg unconsciously rotated his wedding band on his ring finger, looking for his wife Bertha in the crowd of spectators. He spotted her and they exchanged wary smiles.

Judge Van Zile told defense co-council Baxter that he would wait ten more minutes before instructing the bailiffs to return the prisoners to the jail cell adjacent to the court-room. Several minutes passed before Edward Kennedy Jr. walked briskly into the courtroom with Joe and Isadore Burnstein following him. Kennedy settled himself at the defense table while the Burnsteins squeezed into the specta-tor gallery near the jury box.

"My apologies, Your Honor, traffic around the court-house this morning is unusually heavy. I had to park several blocks away and walk in."

Without responding Judge Van Zile brought down the gavel to open the proceedings. "Prosecutor Toy, make your opening statement."

The prosecutor told the jury that the state would prove their case with evidence found at the scene and eyewitness testimony that Raymond Burnstein, Harry Keywell, and Irving Milberg were guilty of the premeditated murder of Joseph "Izzy" Sutker, Joseph Leibowitz, and Herman Paul at the Collingwood Manor Apartments on the afternoon of September 18, 1931.

Defense attorney Edward Kennedy Jr.'s opening remarks to the jury focused sharply on the state's star witness who

Kennedy labeled a sniveling liar who cut a deal with the prosecutors to save his own skin. "Who brings their friends to a massacre and leaves with their killers?" Kennedy asked the jury. "What kind of a person would do that? Ask yourselves, why didn't these accused killers kill Solomon Levine? It doesn't make sense that they would allow him to witness a triple murder and let him live unless he was in on the plan. Levine put the finger on my clients to further his business interests.

"And if that isn't enough, Levine told the police one thing when he was arrested and something else after the prosecutors got ahold of him. He changed his story. Was he lying then or is he lying now? Ask yourselves who will benefit from this travesty of justice. The defense will prove there is only one winner here—Solomon Levine."

The first witness to testify was Detroit Police detective Sergeant William R. McMillan. He and his partner Wallace McRae were the first police on the scene. McMillan testified that Collingwood building supervisor Frank Holt called the Bethune precinct at 3:40 p.m. reporting gunshots fired in apartment 211. When Holt arrived and opened the door with his passkey, he saw three dead men bleeding on the floor. In their cursory search of the apartment, detectives McMillian and McRae found the dead men facedown, each shot numerous times. They also discovered a bucket of green paint under the kitchen sink with three handguns in it. Holt had no knowledge why the paint was there—the murderers brought it with them.

The detectives recognized the dead men and knew they rented rooms at the Orlando Hotel on Brainard Street. McMillian and McRae rushed over to the Orlando and questioned people who resided there and knew the victims.

They quickly discovered Solomon Levine had driven the three murdered men to a meeting at the Collingwood Manor Apartments. That information was the first break in the case. The detectives rushed over to Solly Levine's handbook at Third and Selden and arrested him.

Solly Levine originally told the detectives that some unidentified person held a gun to his back while some other men took the three victims away at gunpoint. Levine claimed they didn't want him and told him to walk into the alley without looking back if he wanted to live. The men drove off in Sutker's car.

On cross-examination, Baxter asked Detective McMillian if he thought twelve hours of police interrogation made Levine change his story and accuse his clients. The Detroit detective was unable to answer; he was only involved with Levine's arrest.

The next witness was Wayne County Coroner Dr. Vincent Mancuso. He had over twenty-five years of experience and had examined hundreds of cadavers who had succumbed to bullet wounds. Dr. Mancuso testified that "sixteen .38-caliber shots were fired, of which fourteen took effect. All were at extremely close range, penetrating the head, chest, and arms. Death was instantaneous; the men bled out after they expired."

Homicide and ballistics detective Max Rickman testified next. The three .38-caliber Colt revolvers found in a bucket of green paint were the murder weapons. The paint was cleaned from the revolvers destroying any fingerprint evidence. An attempt was made to file off the guns' serial numbers, but forensic investigators were able to bring out faint impressions legible enough to read. The guns were traced to a Colt gun factory shipment stolen from a freight car the previous year. There was no way to link the guns to the specific defendants. The defense was pleased.

Assistant Prosecutor Miles Cullehan asked Detective Rickman, "Is it possible to link the guns to the murders?"

"Very possible using ballistics," Rickman answered.

"Would you explain the science of ballistics to the court?"

"It has been proven that every gun has a unique signature. When a bullet is fired, the firing pin leaves a unique impression on the bottom of the metal jacket. The barrel has raised spiral ridges called lands and grooves cut inside the barrel to spin the bullet as it leaves the barrel. When fired, the soft lead of the bullet spins from biting into the rifling in the gun barrel, leaving a unique signature or marks on the slug."

"What is the purpose of the lands and grooves, Dr. Rickman?"

"The spinning makes the bullet more accurate."

"Were you able to match the guns to bullets found in the victims?" Assistant Prosecutor McRae asked.

"Yes, our lab guys were."

"How?"

"We took the bullet evidence from the three victims and matched the rifling with the test bullets we shot from the weapons we found on the scene. The test bullets were recovered from a water tank specially designed for this purpose. Then, we took the brass jackets from the handguns and compared them to the brass jackets fired from the same guns."

"Did they match?"

"Exactly."

"Is there anything else of significance you can tell the court?"

"Yes, there were three victims and three guns used. We were able to determine that each victim was shot with only one of the guns."

Edward Kennedy Jr. took over the cross-examination from his co-council. "Did you find any evidence, Dr. Rickman, linking my clients with these weapons?"

"No, sir." The defense decided to cut its losses. "No further questions, Your Honor."

The defense scored again with Prosecutor Toy's direct examination of Edward Crimmins—Detroit Police fingerprint expert.

"Were there any fingerprints found in the apartment?"

"Lots of them, but they were all smeared."

"Did you examine the front door knob for prints?"

"No."

"Why not?"

"A brass doorknob of that type doesn't show fingerprints."

"What type is that?"

"A fancy one with a design stamped into it. Besides, there was no use taking fingerprints on a door knob used by twenty-five policemen who arrived on the scene before I got there."

"Did you examine the bathroom and the kitchen counters for prints? What about the sink faucets and the stove?"

"We dusted for prints but couldn't find one good enough to photograph. Detectives were touching and leaning on everything."

"So, you found absolutely no fingerprints in the whole apartment?"

"None identifiable."

"Thank you, Mr. Crimmins. No further questions, Your Honor."

"Your witness, counselor."

"No questions, Your Honor," Baxter said from the defense table.

"So far, so good," Baxter whispered to Kennedy as he sat down.

Day one of the trial was a mixed bag. The next day, the defense would go to work on Solomon Levine and try to discredit his testimony on the stand.

The public's attention was focused on this case and they couldn't wait to read the reports in the evening newspapers. The Collingwood Massacre trial thrust the Purple Gang into celebrity status. Everyone in the Detroit area was aware of the case and followed it closely.

———

The second day of the trial had the prosecution's star witness enter the courtroom surrounded by eight burly homicide squad detectives. Solomon Levine was in mortal fear for his life. For their part, Ray Burnstein, Irving Milberg, and Harry Keywell riveted their stares on Levine as did Abe, Joe, and Isadore Burnstein from the gallery.

Prosecutor Toy began questioning his eyewitness. "Mr. Levine, how long have you lived in Detroit?"

"I'm a native Detroiter."

"Where do you live?"

"The Fort Wayne Hotel."

"How old are you?"

"Thirty."

"Where did you go to school?"

"I went to Bishop's and then Fisher and Capron in Paradise Valley. I graduated from Cass Tech. Then, I earned an accounting degree at Detroit Business College."

"Did you ever practice your profession?"

"For six or seven years, I was an accountant for my father's scrap metal business."

"What attracted you to the gambling business?"

"The money and the fast life. I was bored with my job."

"How long have you been running a sports book, Mr. Levine?"

"About four months, I formed a partnership with Izzy Sutker. We opened a handbook on Selden Avenue."

"How long have you known Joseph Sutker and the other victims?"

"A couple of years."

"What other business have you done with this group known as the Little Jewish Navy?"

"A little bootlegging and then some liquor cutting which was less risky."

"Have you ever been arrested or jailed?"

"Never."

"How long have you known the Burnsteins?"

"Objection, Your Honor," defense attorney Baxter interrupted. "That question is prejudicial. Only one Burnstein is on trial here."

"Sustained."

Levine shifted uncomfortably on the stand not making eye contact with anyone. "Mr. Levine, how long have you known Raymond Burnstein?" Prosecutor Toy continued.

"Fifteen years. We hung out together as kids. We went to school together."

"How long have you known Irving Milberg?"

"Five years maybe."

"You're not sure?"

"Sorry, I didn't keep records of when I met people."

"What about Harry Keywell?

"Maybe ten years."

"Have you ever had a problem with any of the defendants?"

"No, we're friends."

"How did you find yourself at the Collingwood Manor Apartments on the afternoon of September 18, 1931?"

"I was a go-between to resolve a problem between the men over an unpaid loan. I was friendly with both groups, so I acted as a peacemaker."

"What can you tell the court about this unpaid loan?" the prosecutor asked.

"In August, Sutker borrowed $13,000 worth of alcohol from Ray Burnstein, which Sutker sold at a profit. Then the handbook had a bad month, so we used the profits to pay off bets. Otherwise, we'd be marked lousy and out of business."

"Did Ray Burnstein threaten Sutker or the other victims?"

"Objection!" Baxter said. "The answer calls for hearsay testimony, Your Honor."

Sol Levine gazed at his lap to avoid eye contact.

"Your Honor, the question begs a simple response. Mr. Levine surely knows if Mr. Sutker told him of a threat."

"Overruled, Mr. Baxter. Answer the question, Mr. Levine."

"No, sir, I ran into Ray on the street, and the unpaid loan came up in conversation, but no threats were made."

"Where did this conversation occur?"

"In front of Levinson's restaurant on Woodward near Temple."

"Were you a party to the loan?"

"No, but Ray knew Sutker and me ran a sports book together."

"Who brought up the subject of the loan?"

"I did. Sutker wanted me to ask Ray for more time, so I took the opportunity."

"What was his reaction?"

"Ray seemed in good spirits and said he had a deal he wanted to work out with the boys. He said, 'Everything is all right. I'll call you in a day or two.'"

"That was it?"

"Yes, Ray called me at the handbook a couple of days later at 2:00 p.m."

"What did Ray Burnstein say?"

"He asked me to bring Sutker, Leibovitz, and Paul to the Collingwood Apartments at 3:00 p.m. on September 18th to work out the conditions to repay the loan. Ray said he had a business offer for them."

"About what?"

"The wine brick business. Ray wanted them to also handle that business."

Prosecutor Toy wasn't sure what the wine brick business was, but he wanted to steer the questioning back toward the crime at hand. "So that was the bait?"

"Sure. I guess so," Levine said.

"How did everyone get to the meeting?"

"I drove them over in Sutker's Desoto and parked out front."

"Please tell the court what happened after you went into the apartment."

"We entered the lobby and looked around. Everything seemed fine, so we climbed the stairs to the second floor. I knocked on the door of apartment 211, and Burnstein opened it inviting us in. He brought Irving Milberg, Harry Keywell, and Harry Fleisher with him. They were seated in the living room on chairs taken from the kitchen which was being painted. The men stood up and everyone shook hands. Reassured, the four of us sat on the couch."

"Did anything seem wrong to you?

"Objection, Your Honor," defense attorney Kennedy said. "The answer calls for an opinion."

"Sustained, counselor."

"What happened next, Mr. Levine?" Toy asked.

"Burnstein said him and his brothers were going legit and wanted to farm out some of their wholesale liquor business to pursue other business opportunities. To sweeten the deal, he also talked about giving the boys the counterfeit liquor label business. But first, he wanted his money."

"Did he strong-arm the men?"

"No. Sutker explained they would pay the loan with profits made during the American Legion Convention the following week. Ray said they were already two weeks late, so they would have to come up with more interest on the loan."

"How did Sutker react to that?"

"He asked Burnstein for the final figure. Burnstein turned to Milberg. 'Where's Scotty with the books, Irving?' Milberg shrugged. 'Go down to the corner drugstore and call him.' Burnstein said he'd be right back and left."

"What happened next, Mr. Levine?"

Everyone in the courtroom listened with rapt attention.

"We made some small talk for about five minutes, when a car horn started blaring and began to race its motor in the alley."

"And what was the significance of that, Mr. Levine?"

"That was a signal for the three gunmen to stand and start firing," Levine said covering his eyes as if trying to erase the image from his mind. "Fleisher fired first. He shot Leibovitz; Keywell shot Sutker; and Milberg shot Paul."

"Did Burnstein shoot anybody?"

"No, but he planned the ambush and was the wheelman."

"What was your role?"

"I was the patsy—the fall guy. Burnstein duped me into bringing the boys to the killing ground."

"Objection! That answer assumes facts not in evidence, Your Honor," Baxter bellowed.

"Rephrase the question, prosecutor."

"Was Ray Burnstein a witness to the shooting?"

"No."

"Did he go to the drugstore to make a call?"

"Apparently not."

"Before you elaborate further, Mr. Levine, what happened after the shooting?"

"Fleisher asked me if I'd been hit. I said, 'No, but bullets whizzed past my face.' He said, 'Come on, come on quick.' The killers dropped their guns in a bucket of paint in the kitchen. We rushed down the stairs and ran into the alley. Ray was behind the wheel of the getaway car. After we jumped in, Burnstein sped out of the alley so fast we narrowly missed a truck on Twelfth Street."

"Where did you go?"

"Burnstein dropped Fleisher and Milberg off several

blocks away. Then, he went a few blocks further and dropped me off, giving me some money for cab fare back to my sport's book. As I was getting out of the car, a gun dropped on the car floor. Keywell ordered me to pick it up, leaving my fingerprints on it. Then, Ray Burnstein said, 'You're my pal, Solly. We'll send a car for you later.' Fifteen minutes later, I was back at my joint. Half an hour later, the police arrested me."

"No further questions, Your Honor."

———

After the lunch recess, defense attorney Edward Kennedy Jr. began his cross-examination. "Mr. Levine, is the testimony you gave the court this morning your only version of events that occurred on the afternoon of September sixteenth?"

"When I gave my first statement to police, I panicked. Knowing what happens to stool pigeons, I told the detectives we were kidnapped by a group of unknown men with handguns. I said one of the gunmen waved me off with a pistol in his hand. 'We don't want you, blow!' he said, so I ducked into an alley as the men loaded Sutker, Leibovitz, and Paul into the back seat of Sutker's car. That's the last time I saw them."

"That was a lie, wasn't it?"

"Yes. I was in a tight spot. I had just witnessed the murders of my friends who were sitting beside me. Bullets were whizzing by my face. I was in shock and panicked. I didn't know what else to do."

"What made you change your story?"

"Detective Sergeant McMillan wasn't buying my alibi.

He told me I had been identified by witnesses that I was on the scene and left with the Purples in the getaway car—a black Chrysler sedan."

"So, why should this court believe you now when you've admitted you lied to police?"

Levine simply shrugged.

Judge Van Zile instructed the witness to answer the question verbally, so the court reporter could record his answer.

"Because it's the truth."

"God's truth or your truth, Mr. Levine?" Kennedy retorted.

"Objection, Your Honor," Prosecutor Toy said.

"I'll withdraw the question. Did the prosecution cut a deal with you for your testimony here today?"

"No, sir."

"Were you offered immunity from prosecution to testify against my clients?"

"No, sir, I wasn't charged with the crime."

"Then what made you change your story?"

"Detective McMillan said if I stuck with my first story, he would recommend to the prosecutor that I be charged with perjury. He told me regardless of my story my survival on the street would be a matter of days if not hours. The killers were facing life in prison for first-degree murder, and they couldn't afford to let me live. I was a marked man."

"What else did they offer you other than immunity?"

"I wasn't offered immunity."

"Then what did they offer you?"

"Police protection and protective custody."

"Anything else?"

"Yes, they offered to smuggle me out of town after the trial."

"Your Honor, the defense moves that this case be dismissed because of the tainted testimony of the witness. He is an admitted liar trying to cut a deal for himself."

"Motion denied," Judge Van Zile ruled. "Are you finished questioning the witness, Mr. Kennedy?"

"Yes, Your Honor, no further questions."

Although Levine appeared pale and tense throughout the entire examination, the defense failed to tear down his story. If Levine was certain of his facts, he answered yes or no. If he wasn't certain, he did not hesitate to admit he didn't know. Levine was unwavering in his attitude, despite the defendants glaring at him throughout his testimony. Ray Burnstein could be seen grinding his teeth and stiffening his jaws. Not once during his testimony did Levine look at the defendants. At the end of the day, Levine appeared relieved to return to the safety of his cell.

On the third day of the trial, the jury, lawyers, and the heavily guarded defendants went to the crime scene to tour the apartment and back alley. The judge wanted the jury to have some visual context before they heard the testimony of other witnesses. The jurors were taken to the Collingwood Manor Apartments on a Detroit city bus with an escort of five police cars forming a front and rear guard. The accused defendants traveled from the Wayne County Jail to the crime scene in a Detroit Police "paddy wagon" under an armed guard.

The defendants were manacled—Burnstein to Keywell and Milberg to a burly detective. They wore no hats or overcoats on this brisk morning. The men were ushered into the apartment through the alley entrance from which the prosecution contended the Purples made their escape.

The jurors stood in the apartment silently waiting for the defendants to arrive. The furniture had been rearranged the way it was on the day of the murders. When the three defendants arrived, the jurors felt uncomfortable standing so near them. The three men betrayed no sign of emotion. All the established details of the murder were pointed out to the jury—the placement of the bodies in the apartment, the location under the kitchen sink of the bucket of green paint, and the placement of the getaway car in the alley. The visitation lasted twenty minutes. Judge Van Zile declared a lunch recess until 1:00 p.m. The jurors were taken to an undisclosed location for lunch rather than the usual institutional food brought to them in the jury room.

———

After court reconvened, Prosecutor Toy introduced into evidence the three .38-caliber Colt revolvers used in the triple slaying. Also introduced were bullets taken from the crime scene and the bucket of green paint. Detective Rickman was recalled to the stand to authenticate the exhibits as those found at the crime scene without objection from the defense.

Prosecutor Cullehan addressed the judge. "Your Honor, the state would like to call Mr. Harry McDonald to the stand."

McDonald came forward and settled uncomfortably into the witness chair.

"Would you identify yourself briefly and tell how you are connected with this case, Mr. McDonald?"

"I'm the apartment manager across the alley from the Collingwood apartments. I was standing at my kitchen sink when I heard a car horn honking and some guy gunning his engine. I opened my window to look into the alley to tell him to knock it off. Then, I heard a volley of pistol shots. Shortly after, I saw four well-dressed men run into the alley from the Collingwood. They jumped into the back seat of a black Chrysler sedan. Then, they sped out of the alley."

"Did you get a good look at the men?"

"No, they were wearing hats. But I did get a good look at the driver."

"Do you see that man in this courtroom this afternoon?"

"Yes, I think so."

"Not certain?"

"No, I see him."

"Mr. McDonald, would you approach that man and place your hand on his shoulder?"

The spectators in the courtroom were transfixed as McDonald approached the defense table and tapped Ray Burnstein on the shoulder before returning to the stand.

"Let the record show that Mr. McDonald identified Raymond Burnstein as the man behind the wheel of the getaway car," the judge directed the court recorder.

"Mr. Kennedy, your witness."

"Mr. McDonald, how far away from the car would you say you were?"

"Maybe twenty feet or so, I guess."

"You're not sure? A man's freedom may be in the balance."

"I don't know the exact distance, but it was close enough for me to see the driver."

"How can you be sure what you heard in the alley wasn't the car backfiring?"

"I'm familiar with the sound of gunfire."

"Are you a hunter, Mr. McDonald?"

"God no!"

"Then how can you be sure what you heard were gunshots?"

"I was a frontline infantry sergeant in Uncle Sam's army overseas. I've heard and fired enough weapons to last me a lifetime."

"No further questions, Your Honor," Kennedy said, hoping the identification of Ray Burnstein by the witness hadn't hurt his client too badly in the eyes of the jury.

"If it please the court, Your Honor, would you call Mr. Frank Holt to the stand?" Assistant Prosecutor Cullehan asked.

"Mr. Holt, please take the stand."

Holt approached the stand, holding his hat by the rim as he was being sworn in.

"Please identify yourself for the jury and your connection to this case."

"I'm the building supervisor of—"

"Would you speak a little louder, Mr. Holt?" the judge asked.

"I'm the building supervisor of the Collingwood Manor Apartments."

"Would you tell the court what you saw and heard the day of the murders?"

"I heard gunshots coming from apartment 211. When the shooting ended, I looked in the apartment and saw the bodies of three men sprawled out on the floor. Then, I ran to my apartment and called the police."

"Do you know who rented that apartment?"

"A man named James Regis. He wore an expensive fedora and dark-smoked glasses. He told me he was a wholesale clothing salesman who traveled a lot. He rented the apartment the week before the murders and paid sixty dollars for the month. I gave him two sets of keys."

"Did you check the man's identification?"

"No. He was well-dressed and paid cash."

"Is the man who called himself James Regis in this courtroom?"

Again, the spectators listened with rapt attention. Mr. Holt looked at the defendants, then, he looked at the gallery where three more Burnsteins were seated. "I'm sorry but I don't recognize anybody," he said.

"Thank you, Mr. Holt. No further questions."

"Mr. Kennedy, your witness."

"Thank you, Your Honor."

"Did you happen to see any of my clients in your apartment house?"

"Never."

"Has anyone approached you about your testimony today?"

"Yes."

"Who?"

"You and the prosecutor's office."

The gallery chuckled.

"Anyone else, Mr. Holt?"

"No, sir."

"No further questions for this witness, Your Honor."

Kennedy returned to the defense table and winked at

Ray Burnstein. The defendants acknowledged one another with wry grins. They sensed the prosecution's case was starting to unravel as many prior court appearances had for these repeat offenders.

Called next to testify was Mrs. Sadie Niss.

"Mrs. Niss, would you tell the court where you live?" Prosecutor Toy asked.

"Yes, I live in the apartment beneath the death flat."

"Do you live there alone?"

"No, I live there with my husband and baby."

"On the day of the murders, please tell the court what you experienced that afternoon."

"I had just put my baby into her crib for a nap when I heard some people walking around upstairs. Then a car parked near the alley door began honking its horn. I heard about twenty loud gunshots that startled me and set my baby crying. I heard three thuds above which sounded like the ceiling would fall in. I was scared and snatched up my baby. I ran into the hall for the cellar. A tall, dark man came running down the stairs and bumped into me, pushing us aside. I asked, 'What's going on?'"

"Did he answer you?"

"No."

"He ran outside and jumped in a waiting car that roared away."

"Were you able to get a look at him, Mrs. Niss?"

"No, sir."

"Were you asked to view a lineup of possible suspects?"

"Yes, I was taken to the police station."

"Do you see anybody in the courtroom who was in that police lineup?"

"Yes."

"Can you point them out?"

"Yes, the three defendants."

"Were any of these men the person who pushed you and your child out of the way?"

"No, sir. He was taller than they are."

"What did you do after the police questioned you?"

"I went to my apartment and tried to put my baby down for a nap."

"Did you notice anything out of the ordinary when you returned to your apartment?"

"Yes, sir, blood had seeped through the floor boards above and soaked through to my ceiling."

"No further questions for this witness, Your Honor. Thank you."

Since Sadie Niss was unable to identify any of the men at the defense table as the person who pushed her and her baby out of the way, her testimony corroborated earlier testimony that there was a fourth man involved who remained at large. There was nothing to be gained by cross-examining this witness, so the defense declined to question her. The judge adjourned court for the day.

———

The first witness on the fourth day of the trial was the driver of the truck the getaway car almost collided with when it sped out of the alley. Larry Pollack was a scrap metal dealer who lived nearby. He went to school with Ray Burnstein and also knew the other defendants. When investigators first questioned Pollack, he identified Burnstein as the driver of the car. But in court that morning he changed his story and testified he saw a dark-complexioned, Latin-type man driving the car. Pollack contradicted Solomon

Levine and Harry McDonald's testimony that Raymond Burnstein was the getaway car driver. Prosecutor Harry S. Toy bore down on the witness with a sharp exchange.

"Your Honor, I request that Mr. Pollack be designated a hostile witness?"

"So noted, counselor."

"Would you explain the charge of 'perjury' for the witness and the penalty in Michigan courts, Your Honor?"

"Perjury is a crime against justice, Mr. Pollack, because it compromises the integrity of the legal system by corrupting it with lies and deceit. When a duly sworn witness who has taken an oath makes a knowingly false statement in a legal proceeding, he or she may be imprisoned for up to fifteen years."

Toy continued. "Didn't you tell me before the trial that I could send you up for perjury, but you wouldn't testify against these defendants?"

Before the witness could answer, both defense attorneys jumped to their feet, objecting.

"That's highly prejudicial to my clients," Kennedy said.

"We demand a mistrial!" Baxter clamored.

The judge did his best to calm the attorneys. Van Zile sustained Kennedy's objection and instructed the court reporter to strike Mr. Toy's question from the record and for the jury to disregard it. Then, he overruled Baxter's mistrial motion. The tension in the courtroom was thick.

"Continue, Mr. Toy."

"What did I tell you when you came to my office to discuss your testimony, Mr. Pollack?"

"You told me if I didn't testify against them, you would send me up for life."

Laughter filled the courtroom and the defendants

smiled. For the first time during the trial, the defendants relaxed.

"Did you go to attorney Kennedy's office with a friend to discuss this case?"

"No, I went there myself at Kennedy's request."

"Weren't you brought there by Joseph Burnstein—the brother of Ray Burnstein?"

"Absolutely not!"

"We have documented proof that you and Joe Burnstein were in Kennedy's office together that morning."

"I did see Joe in Kennedy's office, but it didn't have anything to do with me or the case. We didn't go there together. I briefly said hello and shook his hand. That's it."

"What did you tell defense attorney Kennedy about this case that morning?"

"The truth. I didn't want to get shot up by foreigners."

"Please describe what you told Mr. Kennedy for the record, Mr. Pollack."

"Objection, Your Honor. That violates attorney/client privilege."

"Sustained, Mr. Kennedy. Mr. Toy, rephrase the request as a question."

"Mr. Pollack, would you please tell the court what happened on the afternoon in question?"

"I was driving south on Twelfth Street when a car swung out of the alley and almost collided with my truck. The driver was a dark-complexioned foreigner."

"Do you remember the make or model of the car?"

"It was a black coupe. That's all I remember about it. Everything happened so fast."

"Isn't it true that you told police on the scene that Ray Burnstein was the driver?"

"No! The police tried to get me to say that. They wouldn't take no for an answer. I told them I went to school with Ray Burnstein and it wasn't him."

"Did you tell Inspector John Navarre you knew who the driver was but wouldn't say so?"

"No."

"That's what Inspector Navarre wrote in his initial report."

"If he did, he got it wrong. The police questioned me for eight or nine hours threatening to lock me up the whole time. They were angry I wouldn't repeat their lies."

"No further questions, Your Honor," Toy said, showing disgust with the witness.

Baxter rose and walked to the witness stand.

"Mr. Pollack, did your interrogators threaten you with physical violence at any time during your interview?"

"They gave me the third degree. They were aggressive with me but didn't get physical."

"The police wanted you to implicate my client, Ray Burnstein. Is that what you are saying?"

"Objection, defense counsel is putting words in the witness's mouth."

"Sustained."

"Did you tell the police that Ray Burnstein was not the driver of the car?"

"Yes, sir."

"Who did they want you to say was driving the car?"

"Sol Levine."

"Did you implicate him?"

"No, sir."

"No further questions, Your Honor."

Harry Little was called to the witness stand next.

"Mr. Little," Prosecutor Toy began, "identify yourself and tell the court what your connection is to this case,"

"I'm an interior decorator who was working in a second floor apartment across the alley from the Collingwood the day of the killings."

"Mr. Little, please tell the court what caught your attention that afternoon."

The defendants and their lawyers focused intently on Harry Little's testimony.

"I heard some gunshots coming from the Collingwood and ran to the kitchen. I opened the window that faces the alley and poked my head out. I saw four people run out of the apartment building and jump into a black car before it sped out of the alley."

"Do you know the make and model of the car?"

"It was a black coupe, but I don't know the make."

Prosecutor Toy asked, "Do you recognize anyone in this courtroom who was in that car?"

"Yes, I think so."

"Walk over and point them out, please."

"I only recognize one," Little said reluctantly rising from the witness stand. He walked to the defense table and pointed at Harry Keywell.

When he returned to the stand, Toy asked him, "Where was Mr. Keywell seated in the car, Mr. Little?"

"He was the driver."

The gallery gasped.

"Do you swear to that, Mr. Little?"

"Yes."

"From the second-floor window, are you certain you got a good look at him?"

"Yes, I remember because he had a long jaw which made him stand out."

"No further questions for this witness, Your Honor."

Toy pursed his lips while the defendants smirked.

"Your witness, Mr. Kennedy."

The defense lawyers looked pleased. "No further questions for this witness."

"You're excused, Mr. Little," Judge Van Zile said.

The prosecution asked the judge for a lunch recess before the next witness—fourteen-year-old Herbert Joppick—was called to testify. The boy's mother was bringing him to the court's afternoon session so he wouldn't lose out on a whole day of school.

"Court is adjourned until 1:00 p.m.," the judge said as the gavel came down.

It seemed apparent to the prosecution that someone got to Pollack and Little. They hoped their next witness had not been intimidated into changing his testimony. If he had, the defendants might be acquitted. The prosecutors also worried that despite sequestering the jurors, some of them might have been tainted by individuals sympathetic to the defendants. The defense needed only one juror to hold out for the judge to declare a hung jury. Toy and his assistant prosecutor—Miles Cullehan—waited anxiously to see what the afternoon session would bring.

Fourteen-year-old Herbert Joppick was sworn in and appeared frail and out of place sitting on the stand in the packed courtroom. The thin, blue-eyed, blond-haired teenager was dressed in a blue suit that looked large on him unlike the finely tailored suits the defendants wore.

"Good afternoon, Herbert. Sorry to take you out of school today," Prosecutor Toy said.

"That's okay. I'm going to write an essay about this for my English class."

A good-natured laugh broke out in the gallery. It was a welcome relief after the contentious morning session. Joppick smiled and relaxed on the stand.

"Where do you live, Herbert?"

"The apartment building across the alley from the Collingwood."

"What were you doing in the alley on the afternoon of Wednesday, September sixteenth?"

"It was afterschool and I was in the alley waiting for my little brother."

"Tell the court what you saw, Herbert."

"I heard this guy making a lot of racket with his car in the alley. It kind of echoed between the buildings. Then I heard what I though was the car's engine backfiring. Shortly after, some men hopped into the car."

"Do you remember the make and model of the car you saw?"

"Sure, a black Chrysler sedan. It looked brand new."

Toy paused briefly before he asked the next question. "Can you identify anyone at the defense table as the driver of the car?"

"Yes, I think so."

"You're not sure?"

"Yes. I saw him good when the car shot past me in the alley."

"Would you stand up and walk beside me to the defense table?"

"Okay."

Toy led Joppick to the defendants' table.

"Would you point the driver out, please?"

"Him," Joppick said, pointing to Ray Burnstein.

Burnstein scowled.

Toy returned the teenager to the stand and thanked him.

"No further questions, Your Honor.

"Your witness, counselors," Judge Van Zile said to the defense.

"No questions, Your Honor," Baxter responded.

The defense wanted Joppick off the stand as fast as possible. Baxter did not want the jury to feel empathy for the teen or alienate them with an aggressive cross-examination.

Joppick did his civic duty and left the courtroom with his mother as soon as his testimony was over.

Friday's court session consisted of the prosecution calling two Detroit police investigators to the stand—detectives Thomas Wysockl and George McCellan. Both men impeached the testimony of Larry Pollack, who changed his story on the stand. The defense tried to compromise the detectives by inferring they had given Pollack the third degree, but they were both experienced court witnesses and were unmoved by the allegation.

After the detectives' testimony, the prosecution moved that a bench warrant with the charge of perjury be issued for Larry Pollack."

"Objection!" Baxter bellowed.

"Overruled, Mr. Baxter."

"The prosecution rests its case, Your Honor," Toy said.

It was now time for the long-awaited defense case. Edward Kennedy Jr. and Rodney Baxter decided at the onset of the case not to put their clients on the stand to prevent self-incrimination. That they chose not to call any defense witnesses surprised everyone including the judge.

"The defense rests, Your Honor."

The gallery gasped.

"Would the attorneys approach the bench?" Judge Van Zile asked.

The four lawyers stood before the judge as he spoke in hushed tones.

"Mr. Kennedy and Mr. Baxter, this is quite a surprise to the court."

"The prosecution called every witness, Your Honor, there is nobody left to call."

Toy and Cullehan stood mute.

"Are both sides prepared to give your summations after the lunch recess—to be finished on Saturday if necessary?"

"The prosecution is ready," Toy said.

"The defense needs more time to prepare our summation, Your Honor," Baxter said.

"Any objections, gentlemen," the judge asked the prosecutors, "if I cancel the afternoon session and give the defense the weekend to prepare their final arguments for Monday morning?"

"None, Your Honor," Toy answered.

"Good! That will free up some time so I can issue the bench warrant for Pollack this afternoon."

"Thank you, Your Honor."

The defense did not react. The issuance of the perjury warrant only proved their assertion that Larry Pollack was being persecuted by the prosecution.

"Return to your respective tables, gentlemen."

Judge Van Zile addressed the jury. "The court will adjourn early for the day to give the attorneys time to prepare their final arguments for Monday. Then—after I give you my jury instructions—I will hand the case over to you, so you can begin your deliberations. Court is adjourned until 9:00 a.m. Monday."

—17—

The Collingwood Verdict

AFTER WHAT MUST HAVE seemed like a particularly long weekend for defendants, Judge Van Zile called his courtroom to order promptly at 10:00 a.m. The spectators' gallery was packed to capacity, and the defense lawyers sat like bookends on both sides of their clients. Looking rested and ready for battle, Prosecutor Toy approached the jury box for his summation.

"Ladies and gentlemen of the jury, the task you have before you calls for the judgement of guilt or innocence against these defendants—Raymond Burnstein, Harry Keywell, and Irving Milberg—accused of murdering three men who were their partners in crime. These were cold-blooded, premeditated murders. The killers laid in wait for their victims lured to the Collingwood Manor Apartments by the promise of Ray Burnstein to expand their territory and allow them to handle more of the illegal liquor trade. The victims were known to the police as the Little Jewish Navy, and they were no Boy Scouts. But that doesn't justify their murders by these known Purple Gang members—each with a long arrest record.

"The flat where the murders took place was hired for the express purpose of luring the victims to their deaths. The killers threw their guns in a bucket of green paint they carried there for that express purpose of frustrating fingerprint identification. That shows premeditation. Solomon Levine's whole eyewitness testimony against these killers is wholly unimpeachable. After greeting these victims and inviting them to their deaths, Raymond Burnstein left the apartment on the pretext of making a phone call when in reality he went into the alley, blew his car horn, and raced his car's motor making it backfire to signal the assassins to strike.

"The prosecution has produced every witness connected with this case we knew about, whether they were favorable to our case or not. That is our duty. Three eyewitnesses—Solomon Levine, Harry MacDonald, and Herbert Joppick—who had no reason to lie—place Ray Burnstein behind the wheel of the getaway car. MacDonald and Joppick also testified they saw four well-dressed men run out of the building and hop inside a car before it sped out of the alley.

"A fourth witness—Larry Pollack—initially identified Ray Burnstein at the wheel of the car when it almost ran into his salvage truck. By the time he got to court, he changed his story and blamed an unnamed foreigner. Pollack said the police tried to railroad him into naming Burnstein. Don't be fooled by that. Then, there was Harry Little, the interior decorator who testified he looked out of a second-floor window and saw someone else in the driver's seat. He pointed to Harry Keywell as that person—another defendant in this case. But at the inclined angle of his vantage point, he may have made an honest mistake. That's for you to decide.

"Police crime technicians were able to scientifically match the bullets found in the victims with the three guns found at the murder sight. They were able to corroborate Solomon Levine's testimony that each shooter shot a single victim. We were not able to determine ownership of the three .38-caliber Colt revolvers because the serial numbers were filed off—which again shows premeditation. Lab technicians were able to bring up the numbers enough with a special acid wash to track them to the Colt factory. Company officials cross-checked the numbers and discovered the guns were hijacked from a train car shipment last year. Somehow, those guns showed up at this crime scene. How did they get there? They didn't walk there by themselves. Assassins with murderous intent brought them. We ask you to use your common sense. These men checked their books with bullets and marked off their accounts in blood. They lured their victims to the apartment with promises of partnership, and they killed the men while they were unarmed and helpless.

"The fact that the defense attorneys chose not to place their clients on the stand should not be construed as guilt. That is their right. How curious is it that the defense brought no case in support of their clients? No alibi witnesses and no character witnesses. Not a single one. The defense attorneys will attempt to base their case on further discrediting Solomon Levine. Remember that Mr. Levine was fearful for his life and traumatized by the defendants in the courtroom—not to mention other gang members sitting in the spectators' gallery.

"The defense may try to convince you to bring a lesser charge against Ray Burnstein; after all, they may say, he didn't kill any of these men. But Ray Burnstein planned the murders, set up his associates, and drove the getaway car. That makes him an accessory before and after the fact and as guilty as the men who pulled the trigger.

"Ladies and gentlemen of the jury, if the testimony in this case shows beyond all reasonable doubt that Raymond Burnstein, Harry Keywell, and Irving Milberg are guilty, you must return a first-degree murder verdict." Prosecutor Toy paused and looked at the jury. "Thank you."

Edward Kennedy Jr. rose from behind the defense table with a big smile and addressed the jury. The defense strategy was to attack Solomon Levine and his testimony hoping to win an acquittal for their clients. If Kennedy could convince even one juror to hold out and vote not guilty, the judge would have to declare a hung jury and retry the case with a new jury.

"After a solid week of testimony, it's come down to this, ladies and gentlemen of the jury. It is your legal responsibility to decide the fate of Raymond Burnstein, Harry Keywell, and Irving Milberg. You must decide the guilt or innocence of my clients based on every witness—not just those who help the prosecution's case.

"First, let me ask you, who benefits the most from these murders and false claims made by Solly Levine? Sol Levine, that's who! He had to implicate somebody or else he would be accused himself. Remember, Levine is a confessed liar. He told police detectives that someone stuck a gun in his back and told him to 'scram' and don't look back before their captors drove off with Isadore Sutker, Joseph Leibowitz, and Hymie Paul. But his kidnapping story doesn't pass the smell test, so he used my clients as a scapegoat for his own complicity.

"Sol Levine instigated these murders because he had a strong motive—personal gain. He would fall heir and sole owner of the Selden Avenue sports book and take a leading role in what the press calls the Little Jewish Navy. Mr. Levine is not a model citizen. He has been a bootlegger, a whiskey cutter, a numbers runner, and now a bookie. What he can add to his other crimes is conspiracy to commit murder. He sought to cancel a debt through the murder of his business associates. And to compound that travesty, he didn't tell the police the names of the real killers but named men to whom he owed money—namely my clients. With them out of the way, Sol Levine and his associates would take over the gang and move in on other rackets. Any other explanation of Levine's story is fantastic and doesn't ring true.

"Fact—Sol Levine stated that he and Burnstein set up the meeting between Sutker, Leibowitz, and Paul to resolve an unpaid loan. Fact—Sol Levine drove the unsuspecting victims to their death. Fact—Sol Levine said he was spared by Ray Burnstein because they were school pals, despite Levine being the only eyewitness to this capital crime. And fact—Sol Levine left the scene of the crime with the accused killers and lived to tell the tale. Don't be fooled by the prosecution. This case just doesn't add up, ladies and gentlemen of the jury.

"Prosecutor Toy failed to prove that Ray Burnstein rented the apartment using the name James Regis. The apartment manager was unable to identify Burnstein as that man. Then there is the matter of fingerprints. The police experts were not able to find any fingerprints because they were stumbling over each other in their investigation destroying evidence. If the police made a careful examination of the fingerprints, they might have gotten the real killers and my clients would be innocent.

"The three murdered men were members of a gang who had been in a hijack war with another local gang. A man named Butler was killed after he and some other men hijacked one of the Jewish Navy's liquor shipments. How is that for a motive? A vendetta—a blood feud. Solly Levine said he thought the meeting with my clients was over a $13,000 loan that was past due. Izzy Sutker owed the money to Burnstein. Would my client kill Sutker, who owed him money before he could pay it back? Not only is that bad business, it's foolish. 'There were other motives at work behind the scenes,' the prosecutor told this court, but they never established what exactly those motives were—a larger piece of the action? Saying so doesn't make it so. The prosecution never made their case, so I ask you, Where is the proof?

"The state is not acting in good faith. The prosecution would have you gloss over the testimony of Larry Pollack—who said in open court under threat of perjury—that Ray Burnstein was not the driver of the slayers' getaway car. Pollack swore the prosecutor and the police threatened to throw him in jail for life if he didn't cooperate and testify against Burnstein. It might interest the jury to know that the prosecution asked for and got a bench warrant signed by the judge last Friday for Mr. Pollack's arrest. The authorities may call it a self-fulfilling prophecy, but the defense calls it judicial harassment and a gross violation of Mr. Pollack's constitutional rights.

"And don't forget Mr. Harry Little's corroborative testimony that the driver of the getaway car wasn't Ray Burnstein. In the prosecutor's summation, Mr. Toy suggested Mr. Little viewed what he saw from a skewed angle and was likely mistaken. How convenient for the state's case! Don't be fooled, ladies and gentlemen of the jury, the prosecution has played fast and loose with the facts of this case from the beginning.

"The defense believes the prosecution has failed to make its case. In their rush to judgement, the police, the prosecution, and the press have created a house of cards to deprive my clients of their freedom—one in particular—Raymond Burnstein. The police have been hounding the Burnstein family for years, but never—not once—has a Burnstein been convicted of charges brought against him. Why? Because they were innocent!

"If any of the testimony you heard last week raises a reasonable doubt in your minds, then, we demand a verdict of not guilty. The defense is confident you will make the right decision and justice will prevail. Thank you."

Court was adjourned for the day. As the gavel came down, Ray Burnstein, Harry Keywell, and Irving Milberg huddled together for a moment and then broke out into audible chuckles. It was the first real sign of relief the defendants displayed since the case began.

The following morning, Judge Van Zile gave his final instructions to the jury.

"You've heard the testimony of the witnesses, law enforcement, and the summations of the attorneys. Now it is your task to weigh the evidence and deliberate on the guilt or innocence of the defendants. You can bring a first-degree murder verdict or a second-degree murder verdict, but you cannot bring a manslaughter verdict. First-degree murder is premeditated with malice aforethought. Second-degree murder requires no premeditation—but malice must be proved. If you have reasonable doubt as to malice, premeditation, or intent, then your verdict should be not guilty. The first thing you need to do before you deliberate is elect a jury foreman. Understood?"

The jury assented by nodding.

Judge Van Zile handed the fate of the three defendants to the jury at 10:19 a.m. on Tuesday, November 10. One hour and thirty-four minutes later, at 11:53 a.m., their deliberations were over. The jury foreman—Steven Howey—sent word to the judge through the bailiff that the jury had arrived at a verdict. When the prosecution and defense attorneys were notified and in place, the defendants were returned to the courtroom. Judge Van Zile asked the bailiff to bring in the jury. Two of the women jurors were in tears, quietly weeping into handkerchiefs as they emerged from the jury room.

"Has the jury reached its verdict?"

Jury foreman Howey stood up. "Yes, Your Honor, we have."

Van Zile instructed the defendants to rise and face the jury.

The court clerk said, "Members of the jury, who speaks for you?"

Steven Howey rose from his seat in the jury box. "I do."

In a clear voice, Howey read the verdict. "We, the members of the jury, find the defendants Ray Burnstein, Irving Milberg, and Harry Keywell guilty of murder in the first degree."

There was a gasp in the courtroom. From the rear of the gallery, Harry Keywell's mother screamed and sobbed loudly. Two police matrons escorted her into the lobby to comfort her as best they could. Keywell's elderly father got up to follow his wife but almost collapsed. He was also helped to the lobby. Mrs. Bertha Milberg—an attractive, dark-haired woman dressed smartly in a tight-fitting black suit with a fashionable black hat—was prepared to warmly embrace her husband on his acquittal. Instead, she was seated five feet behind him in the front row, whimpering in a restrained and dignified manner.

Keywell's face went ashen, Milberg was visibly shaken, but Ray Burnstein stood showing little emotion. Abe, Joseph, and Isadore Burnstein sat dumbfounded in the gallery, and the defense lawyers grimaced in disbelief. The Burnstein brothers' myth of judicial immunity was shattered, and its discordant echoes reverberated throughout Detroit's underworld.

"I wish to thank the jury for their work in this case," the judge said. "It has been a hard, strenuous trial, and your service is appreciated. The court has endeavored to its utmost ability to give a fair and impartial trial, and I believe the jury rendered the correct verdict."

"Judge Van Zile, the prosecution would like to express its thanks to the jury also," Toy said. "

"Please do."

"This verdict is encouraging in the fight against crime in Detroit. The jury is to be congratulated. When we have fearless and honest juries, the criminals' day in this city will be short-lived."

Not to be outdone, defense attorney Baxter announced that an appeal would be filed immediately with the State Court of Appeals to reverse this travesty of justice. Then, he moved that Judge Van Zile sentence the defendants immediately.

"Under the law, Mr. Baxter, I must refer all felony cases to the probation department before sentencing. Sentencing will be next week."

In his closing remarks, Judge Van Zile addressed the convicted felons. "You have established reputations as members of the Purple Gang, which has undoubtedly placed you at the peak of the racketeer in the city of Detroit and has unfortunately brought an unsavory reputation to this fair city. This crime has been a great tragedy, not only as it pertains to you but also because it demonstrates that such a thing could be done in what we call our enlightened age. I declare these proceedings closed," the judge said as he brought the gavel down for the last time.

The convicted men were handcuffed and marched out of the courtroom to be returned to their cells in the Wayne County Jail. Although the penalty for first-degree murder in Michigan was well-known—mandatory life in prison without parole—the formal sentencing was a week away. It would take that long to prepare the paperwork before Judge Van Zile could remand the prisoners to the Michigan Department of Corrections. When all was said and done, the three convicts landed in Marquette Prison in the Upper Peninsula of the state—Michigan's highest security penitentiary for its most dangerous criminals.

—18—

Milford Jones Put on the Spot

MILFORD JONES WAS PART of a contingent of St. Louis contract killers imported into Detroit to flex out-of-town muscle at the behest of the Purple Gang. After his friend and mentor Fred "Killer" Burke was sentenced to life in Marquette Prison, Jones stayed on as a Purple Gang associate and became a well-known and feared triggerman by Detroit's Mafia—some of whom Jones helped run out of St. Louis years before. Several of the old St. Louis Mafia members migrated to Detroit and had since risen to power in the Eastside mob.

For some unknown reason, Jones harbored a personal grudge against Sicilian and Italian gangsters and was reputed to have killed no less than twenty-nine Mafia foot soldiers in his short career. Jones was repeatedly warned by Purple Gang elder Abe Burnstein to stop harassing Mafia-protected speakeasies, gambling joints, and brothels. But Jones wouldn't listen and continued to rob Mafia customers and extort what money he could from Mafia-protected businesses. Jones thought of himself as an independent contractor who was building his own organization—rather than a subordinate Purple Gang associate. This was a fatal miscalculation on his part.

Jones walked alone and unarmed into the Stork Club—a known Purple Gang hangout—at 4:00 a.m. on Wednesday, June 15, 1932. He strode to the bar, placed his right foot on the brass rail and ordered a drink. Looking in the mirror behind the bar, Jones saw four men closing in on him. Before he could turn to face them, he grabbed the lapel of his suitcoat and pulled it across his face. Two triggermen emptied their guns into him—three shots to the brain and more to the body. Jones's right foot got hung up in the brass rail as he went down.

The call came in to the police department at 6:45 a.m.—almost three hours after the murder. Detroit Police found the body lying in a pool of congealed blood. By the time they arrived, all the potential witnesses had scattered—the customers, the bartender, the hat-check girl, the resident blues singer, and the musicians. Only Stork Club owners Jack Greenstein and Peter Gorenfield were there to meet police. Both men were taken to police headquarters for questioning. Neither owner witnessed the killing but provided a list of everyone working the club that early morning. Both owners were released and told not to leave town.

The next day, police rounded up band leader William E. Maschie, musician John Bentenmiller, porter Clyde Hill, blues singer Caroline Snowden, valet Edward Sharp, and bartender Robert Marshall for interrogation. Witnesses positively identified Eastside Mafia lieutenants Peter Licavoli and Joe Massei from police mug shots as the triggermen. Licavoli and Massei both disappeared from Detroit streets only underscoring their involvement. Police suspected Joe

"Scarface" Bommarito and Peter Corrado to be the other men in the group that crowded Jones. The wingmen were also conspicuous by their absence, but eyewitnesses failed to identify either of them, so they were in the clear.

Shortly after the shooting, a local youth found one of the murder weapons near the entrance of the nightclub. The unidentified boy secretly held onto the gun before showing it to a friend who convinced him to turn the weapon over to police. Ballistic tests determined that the gun was one of the murder weapons, but investigators were unable to establish who owned the firearm.

Jones's passing was not particularly mourned at police headquarters, but they worked the case as hard as they could. Frustrated with lack of progress one week after the murder, Detroit and Michigan State Police detectives initiated a sweep of known Mafia hangouts to show they were taking the Jones murder seriously. Two saloons, four nightclubs, three poolrooms, and a supper club were raided. The dragnet yielded fifty-four annoyed Italian gangsters who needed to be fingerprinted, photographed, and identified. Disappointed, it became clear to Prosecutor Duncan C. McCrea that nobody in Detroit was willing to roll over on either Licovoli or Massei.

On Tuesday, June 28, 1932, suspected accessory Joe Bommarito and his lawyer showed up unexpectedly at Detroit police headquarters where the Mafia underboss was told he wasn't wanted for anything and was free to go. Any relief Bommarito may have felt for being in the clear was tempered by the knowledge that an unmarked police car followed his car home, and he was on around-the-clock surveillance until further notice.

Eight months went by until police caught up with Joe

Massei in Detroit on February 2, 1933. Pete Licavoli was arrested in Toledo and extradited to Detroit three months later on May 2, 1933. Almost a year had gone by since the Milford Jones murder. Prosecutor Duncan C. McCrea had trouble locating his eyewitnesses, including Stork Club owner Peter Gorenfield. The judge was forced to dismiss the case. The prisoners were released from custody and nobody seemed to care.

No services were held in Detroit for Jones. His body was returned to his relatives in St. Louis, Missouri, for a family burial at Valhalla Cemetery.

—19—

Abe Axler and Eddie Fletcher
Take a Ride

AFTER THE COLLINGWOOD MANOR Massacre, Detroit authorities began a major crackdown on the underworld and their illicit activities. The Michigan legislature passed the Disorderly Persons Act, which went into effect on September 18, 1931. The idea behind the act was that people who were known criminals or associated with known criminals could be arrested and held for suspicion of criminal activity. Abe Axler was named Michigan Public Enemy number one, and Eddie Fletcher was number two. The pair was rounded up with other alleged Purple Gang members, including gang mentor Charles "the Professor" Auerbach of the defunct Oakland Sugar House Gang. The men were arrested in Auerbach's home where five handguns, a rifle, a stockpile of ammunition, and tear gas bombs were found.

On September 24, 1931, Purple Gang lawyer Edward Kennedy Jr. argued at their arraignment before Recorder's Court Judge Arthur E. Gordon that the Disorderly Persons

Act was unconstitutional because defendants could be convicted on their reputation alone. Judge Gordon suggested Kennedy take it up with the Michigan Supreme Court and set bail at five hundred dollars. Axler and Fletcher were released later that day.

Abe Axler was the first person to be tried under the new Public Enemy law on October 5, 1931, but Axler and Fletcher were charged with crimes that occurred before the Public Enemy law went into effect. Prosecutor Harry S. Toy failed to make his case, and the jury found Axler not guilty on October 10, 1931. Toy was forced to drop the charges on Eddie Fletcher too. Both men had been out of circulation for two years and released recently from Leavenworth Federal Prison after paying their debt to society for violating the Volstead Act. But Charles "the Professor" Auerbach was convicted on October 27, 1931, five weeks after the Public Enemy Law went into effect and was placed on probation and fined a paltry one hundred dollars. That was less than a slap on the hand. The law was soon challenged and found unconstitutional by the Michigan Supreme Court.

Surviving members of the shattered Purple Gang began to strike out on their own and develop new ways of making money. The bottom was about to fall out of the illegal liquor trade with the repeal of Prohibition. The Roaring Twenties were over, and the Great Depression had a choke hold on the economy. Thirty-two-year-old Abe Axler and thirty-five-year-old Eddie Fletcher were broke when released from federal prison. The pair tried to muscle in on Detroit's narcotics trade which was firmly in the grasp of the Mafia and Pete Licavoli's Eastside Gang.

Early Sunday morning on November 26, 1933, Abe Axler and Eddie Fletcher were taken for a ride. Their bodies

were found in the back seat of a new Chrysler sedan licensed
to Evelyn Axler. Each man was shot five times. Fletcher was
shot in the right arm and the left chest, and he took three
to the face from a .38-caliber revolver. Axler was shot five
times to the right side of the head with a .45-caliber automatic pistol. Fletcher, seated on the left, was propped up
against Axler. The men were holding hands. They were virtually inseparable companions in life and called the Siamese
Twins by the underworld. The gesture was meant as a
symbol of disrespect and a slur on their manhood. The only
clues Oakland County Sheriff detectives had were three
spent cartridge casings from the .45 automatic and slugs
taken from the victims' bodies from both guns.

The men were discovered at 2:00 a.m. on Quarton
Road near Telegraph Road—a short mile away from
affluent Bloomfield Township in Oakland County where
many notable crime figures resided. Constable Fred Lincoln
making his nightly rounds came upon the car on the foggy,
gravel road. He approached cautiously and called out but
got no response. He shined his flashlight in the back window
and saw the slaughtered men. Shaken, he went to his nearby
home and called the Oakland County Sheriff. When the
sheriff's men arrived on the scene, Constable Lincoln told
them he passed the intersection at 1:20 a.m. and the car
wasn't there. When he returned at 2:00 a.m., he found the
victims. The murders happened sometime within that forty-
minute window.

Axler and Fletcher were taken to Pontiac General
Hospital morgue where their fingerprints were taken. Mrs.
Evelyn Axler and Mrs. Anna Fletcher were notified by
Detroit police and brought to the hospital to make positive

identifications and claim their husbands' bodies. Both women shrieked at the sight of their husbands' mutilated corpses. Anna Fletcher mumbled, "That's my Eddie. I'll get those rats."

Once the women were able, they told investigators that their husbands had been out of town looking for work and returned early Saturday morning. The two men and their wives shared a two-bedroom flat at 3245 West Chicago Boulevard. Both men were exhausted and slept all day. They woke up and dressed for dinner. As the couples were finishing dinner, the telephone rang. Axler answered the phone like he was waiting for the call. Abe told Eddie they had to go out. The men did not say where they were going, and their wives knew better than to ask. Anna Fletcher cautioned her husband to be careful, and Eddie told her with a smile, "I'm always careful. You know that." Then the men left in Evelyn Axler's new Chrysler touring sedan.

Both Axler and Fletcher were New York transplants well-known to Detroit police. Axler had eighteen arrests to his credit over thirteen years with three convictions. He served two sentences in Sing Sing Correctional Facility and a federal rap in Leavenworth. Fletcher had been arrested eleven times and served only one prison sentence. Fletcher, Axler, and three other Purples served the same sentence for the same crime in Leavenworth. Once arrangements were made by Lewis Brothers Funeral Parlor in Paradise Valley, their bodies were shipped to their birthplace in New York City for burial.

At a press conference, Chief of Detectives Fred Frahm told reporters, "Everything suggests that Axler and Fletcher were murdered at the hands of their own gang. If out-of-town talent was brought in by another gang, the remaining Purple Gang members would be hiding, but this time they are openly walking Detroit's streets."

Wayne County Prosecutor Harvey S. Toy suggested that the gangsters were slain as a reprisal for double-crossing a narcotics ring. The victims were known opium smokers and narcotics dealers. Word on the street was Axler and Fletcher had run afoul of Harry Millman for some real or imagined reason. The dual hit was clearly a two-man job done by someone Axler trusted to drive his wife's new car. Police wondered how the Axlers got the money to buy their new car when neither of them had no visible means of support. After paying their $5,000 fines and serving twenty-two months in Leavenworth, Axler and Fletcher were broke. As far as authorities could surmise, neither man left a large cache of money to provide for their wives. Axler died with $18.60 in his pockets, and Fletcher had 60 cents.

The bodies of both men were shipped to New York for burial. Axler was buried in Brooklyn, King's County, and Fletcher was buried in Elmont, Nassau County. His burial expenses were paid by the First Brodyer B. Benevolent Association.

Nobody was ever charged with their murders, but the result of the crime seriously crippled the Purple Gang. With two of the Purples' most feared killers off Detroit streets, other gangs began to see opportunities. Detroit became a battleground over who would inherit the spoils of the Purple Gang's demise and rule Detroit's underworld.

Abe Burnstein couldn't run his crime empire by himself. His brothers Joe and Isadore were living in California where they became consultants for West Coast gambling concerns, far removed from Detroit's mean streets.

The heyday of the Purple Gang was over. The Twenty-First Amendment repealed the Eighteenth Amendment Prohibition Law on December 5, 1933, with ratification by two-thirds of the states and a joyous proclamation by first-year president Franklin Delano Roosevelt. The only people more upset by the end of Prohibition than members of the Temperance Movement were bootleggers who were suddenly out of a job. Some people got out of the liquor business, while others reopened their speakeasies and blind pigs as legitimate, licensed nightclubs or bars. Times had changed. The Purple Gang's Detroit crime empire was crumbling, but Abe Burnstein still controlled the Purple Gang numbers racket and the horseracing wire service—but not for long.

—20—

The Harry Millman Murder

By THE MID-1930S, THE Purple Gang no longer had an organizational presence on Detroit Streets. Their ranks were decimated by gangland murders and long jail sentences for key members. They no longer had the muscle or the manpower to control their extensive numbers racket and racetrack wire service. To stem a gang war the Purple Gang couldn't win, Abe Burnstein ceded what was left of the gang's rackets to the Eastside Mafia. The Purples had a long history of cooperative relations with the Italians and often worked with them in various schemes and capers. A few diehard Purples tried to form their own crews riding on the Purple Gang name.

By 1935, Harry Millman became known as the lone wolf of the Detroit underworld. Millman formed his own crew and continued to run his own handbook, infiltrate labor unions as "organizers," and shake down Mafia-protected gambling operations, brothels, and nightclubs. Millman had a reputation for out-of-control violence and was known as an angry drunk with a chip on his shoulder.

Millman harbored a grudge against the Mafia and shook down their protected businesses—often pistol-whipping Mafia customers who happened to get in his way. Millman's reputation for ruthless violence made him the most feared enforcer in Detroit's underworld and a prime target for the Mafia's wrath.

Mafia underbosses Pete Licavoli and Joe Bommarito met with Abe Burnstein demanding that Harry Millman be eliminated. Burnstein warned Millman time and again to stop making trouble with the Italians, but he wouldn't listen. In 1936, Millman and Bommarito had a knock-down, drag-out fistfight at Sam Finazzo's Café on Eighth and Fort Streets. Millman came out on top and Bommarito lost face but vowed revenge.

Recent successes in his numbers and handbook rackets made Millman lots of money. He bought a luxury, maroon Cadillac LaSalle V-8 touring sedan, and he began wearing expensive suits. After a night of dining and dancing at the 1040 Club with the wife of Harry Fleischer—whose husband was serving a sentence in Jackson prison—Millman sent Hattie Fleischer home in a cab while he waited for a couple of his men.

At 3:00 a.m., Millman gave the club's valet—Willie W. Holmes—the keys to get his new car. Holmes turned the ignition key exploding seven to ten sticks of dynamite wired to a spark plug. Windows were blown out in nearby build-ings, and burglar alarms were set off which brought police quickly to the scene. The car's hood was found on the roof of the five-story building it was parked next to. Holmes's legs were almost severed as he was blown through the car's rear window. The thirty-nine-year-old valet later died in Receiving Hospital. Within moments of the explosion, over one thousand people jammed around the smoldering wreck. Holmes's death was the first car bomb slaying in Detroit.

After the bombing, Detroit's hotel owners refused to rent Millman rooms for fear he would be murdered in their place of business. Shortly after the attempt on his life, Millman—in a drunken rage—shot up a Mafia-protected brothel. Harry Millman's associates believed he harbored a death wish. Millman began frequenting Boesky's Delicatessen which had a cocktail lounge attached to it. He began going on night-long drinking binges—a habit noticed by his adversaries as they shadowed his movements.

Millman left the scene after the car bombing. The next day, he was summoned by the homicide squad for interrogation. "I decided the best thing for me to do was to scram," he told Deputy Chief Navarre, "so I hired a cab and went to Hamtramck."

"Why Hamtramck?"

"It wasn't Detroit."

Millman was shaken by his close brush with death. He sat fidgeting in his seat, nervously tearing pieces of paper. "I'm as legitimate as the next guy. All I do is run a few handbooks on Twelfth Street, but you cops keep raiding them. I'm getting kicked around like a football. It's a nightmare for me."

"Do you have any idea who put the hit out on you, Harry?"

"No, I haven't been active in the rackets since Prohibition was repealed four years ago. I'm trying to scratch out a living like everyone else. I run a few handbooks—that's all."

"What about someone attempting to settle old scores, Harry? After all, you've got plenty of enemies in this town. Surely you could drop a few names."

"The only people crawling up my ass are you cops."

"What about that labor trouble at the Newton Packing Company you were involved with last month?"

"I had nothing to do with that."

Millman—along with Louis Fleischer and Sam Cooper—led a three-week strike of the Newton Packing Company where $170,000 worth of perishable meats spoiled in trucks before the company settled. The teamsters refused to deliver them or allow anyone else to.

"Then there is this. You were out nightclubbing with Harriet Fleischer. Maybe Louis told his brother Harry in Jackson Prison that you're moving in on his wife."

"Hattie and me are just friends. She's been sad with her husband locked up. I just wanted to cheer her up. She's a good dancer, so we went dancing."

"Right!" Navarre said.

"I sent her home in a cab. Ask the bartender."

"We already did. How would you like to spend a couple of days in the bull pen with the boys, Millman?"

"On what charge?"

"Running illegal sport books."

Millman gave the deputy chief a hard look and tightened his jaw.

"What about the Italian mob? You've been in a running battle with them for two years. Weren't you in a fist fight with Joe Bommarito in Sam Finazzo's place?"

"I've got no business with that grease ball."

"Really. Maybe he has business with you. Licavoli and Bommarito came to see me voluntarily yesterday. Both men claimed they had no information about the car bombing except what they read in the papers."

"Well, you know what stand up guys they are, Navarre."

"So you suspect them?"

"No, I don't have any information either."

"Too bad. That's a real shame."

"Yeah, I can tell you're all broke up about it," Millman quipped.

"Before we release you, tough guy, we'd like to offer you some police protection."

"From the cops? Not a chance."

"It's your call. Just stay out of sight until we solve this murder."

"As long as you stay off of my back, I don't care what you do."

"Nice knowing you, Harry. Good luck!"

Millman left the police station looking over his shoulder for the vengeance he knew would surely come.

———————

On November 25, 1937—early Thanksgiving morning—Harry Millman, Hymie Cooper, and Harry Gross were drinking at a table in Boesky's cocktail lounge just before 1:00 a.m. Millman got up and went to the bar to order more drinks. Two men in dark snap-brim hats and tan polo coats walked from Boesky's adjoining deli, strode up to Millman, and opened fire with two .45-caliber automatic weapons from two feet away. Tough guy Millman was dead before he hit the floor.

Patrons ran for cover as the gunmen emptied their clips randomly around the bar. Four other people were wounded, including Purple Gangster Harry Gross, who died in the hospital several days later. When finished shooting, the gunmen simply put their weapons in their pockets and walked out the front door, got into a waiting Ford sedan, and vanished into the night. One of the gunmen's hats was found on the sidewalk. That was the first clue, which led to a New York haberdashery but no further.

A bystander outside Boesky's Bar wrote down the Michigan license plate number of the getaway car and gave it to police. When the car was recovered, Police found it had a stolen plate. The vehicle identification number led to New York City. The car was registered fictitiously to one Joseph Cohen at the address of a vacant lot. Detroit police were convinced whomever killed Millman and Gross were out-of-towners. Their investigative work was done.

Wayne County Medical Examiner Dr. R. Robert Kollman found ten bullet wounds in Millman's body. All of the bullets passed through his body because of the close range. One bullet severed his spine while others hit him in the center of the forehead, his upper lip, the left side of his neck, his right shoulder, his right wrist, his left arm, his abdomen, and two in the chest. Harry Millman was twenty-seven-years-old when he met his violent end. He still listed his parent's address at 2080 E. Euclid Avenue as his legal residence though he maintained separate quarters at 26 Peterboro Street.

Three days after the murder, the *Detroit Free Press* ran this editorial: "The underworld doesn't bother with jury trials or writs of habeas corpus. Usually, a finger man points out the victim and the gunmen do the rest—so ended the life of Harry Millman. The penalty inflicted upon him cannot be mitigated by an indulgent pardon or parole board. Jungle law cannot be condoned, but the taxpayers do not have to pay for his keep for years in a steam-heated and radio-equipped penitentiary. The real tragedy of this shooting is that bystanders get caught in the line of fire."

New York–based crime reporter Walter Winchell described the hit on his nightly national news program this way:

> In a big Midwest metropolis yesterday, another gang member met justice at the end of a gun. Prominent Detroit Purple Gang member Harry Millman was enjoying a drink in the bar of Boesky's Restaurant on 12th Street when two men entered brandishing hand guns and shot the hoodlum ten times. His body was still warm when the Detroit Police arrived. His killers were rumored to be members of Brooklyn's notorious Murder Incorporated. Millman's death signaled the end of the Purples as a force in organized crime in the Motor City. Because of his repeated escapes from convictions for kidnapping, robbery, and extortion, Millman earned the nickname "Lucky." Yesterday, his luck ran out. This is Walter Winchell reporting.

In 1940 Brooklyn, New York, Murder Incorporated mob figure Abe "Kid Twist" Reles turned state's evidence for District Attorney Thomas E. Dewey outlining the first blueprint of a national crime organization called the Syndicate. Reles testified before under the protection of the New York Police Department that the Detroit Mafia tried unsuccessfully to kill Harry Millman by blowing up his car with him in it. When that failed, Harry "Happy" Malone and Harry "Pittsburgh Phil" Strauss were given a contract by Murder Incorporated to rub out Millman. Though Malone and Strauss never stood trial for Millman's murder, the pair was convicted in New York City for other murders, and both men went to the electric chair in Sing Sing.

While under police protection, stool pigeon Abe Reles fell to his death from the window of a room at the Half Moon Hotel in Coney Island, New York on November 12, 1941. The disposition of the body several feet from the building suggested to forensic investigators that Reles was thrown from the window rather than falling, but his death was ruled an accident by the New York City coroner.

—21—

Purple Gang Epilogue

As far as the Detroit Police Department was concerned, the murder of Harry Millman marked the end of the Purple Gang. No longer would the Purple Gang run roughshod on city streets and compromise the reputation and the integrity of the police force like they had in the 1920s and early 1930s. The Purple Gang's reign of terror—punctuated with bullets and written in blood—was over.

The older and smarter Purples left the rackets to invest in legitimate and semi-legitimate businesses. Twenty-six members of the gang served long prison terms escaping the wrath of rival gunmen. Sixteen of the Purple Gang died at the hands of equally violent criminals—many from within their own ranks. Lack of a strong central leader prompted many of the young Purples, who refused to give up the gang life, to strike out on their own further leading to the gang's implosion.

The Wall Street stock market crash of October 1929 shrank federal tax revenues. Jobs, income, and capital gains disappeared. The increasing cost of enforcing the Prohibition laws prompted two-thirds of the states and the federal government to pass the twenty-first amendment to the Constitution repealing Prohibition in 1933. The country needed revenue to run the government, so an alcohol tax was passed in 1934 that comprised 9 percent of all federal revenue for that year. The return of the alcohol industry created thousands of jobs not only in distilleries and breweries but also in the bottle, cork, barrel making, trucking, and distribution industries. Bars and cocktail lounges were now legal to operate employing bartenders, musicians, waitresses, and cooks.

With the repeal of Prohibition late in 1933, the bottom fell out of the bootlegging business. Abe Burnstein still controlled much of the policy racket (numbers) and the horse-racing subscription wire service, but once his brother Ray was given a life sentence for the Collingwood murders and Joe and Izzy left Detroit to settle in California, Abe made what may be one of the shrewdest moves in underworld history. In a meeting with the leaders of the newly formed Detroit Partnership, Abe cut a deal with bosses Joe Zerilli and William Tocco in 1935 to hand over his gambling empire to them. In return, the Mafia chieftains agreed to maintain Burnstein in his twenty-sixth-floor penthouse suite in the exclusive Book-Cadillac Hotel until his death from heart failure on March 7, 1968, at the age of seventy-seven.

———

By the start of World War II, the Purple Gang was all but forgotten. News of the impending war in Europe dominated the headlines. By the end of the war, the Purple Gang was ancient history to younger Detroiters. The atrocities and terror of the Second World War by comparison made the Purple Gang look like the neighbor thugs they were. But if you or your family were victimized by the Purples, the memories of their terror were still painful regardless of the slow march of time.

A January 24, 1946, FBI office memorandum from a Detroit bureau chief written to Director J. Edgar Hoover made mention of the Purples as "a group of choice racketeers and hoodlums who derived the greater part of their income through bootlegging and the sale of sugar and malt during prohibition days, as well as shakedowns and holdups of gambling houses, bookies, and houses of prostitution. At the present time, the Purple Gang is said to be defunct in Detroit as a criminal organization."

In 1951, Senator Estes Kefauver took his Senate organized crime committee to fourteen American cities in fifteen months to investigate the influence of organized crime on interstate commerce. As the committee moved to Detroit, WWJ-TV preempted *The Howdy Doody Show* and its other daytime programming to broadcast senators grilling mobsters and politicians live on television for three days. Thirty-five people were called in Detroit to testify, including Michigan Governor G. Mennen Williams, Detroit Mayor Albert E. Cobo, Detroit Police detectives, state police spokespersons, Ford Motor Company Security Chief Harry Bennett, and well-known Detroit underworld figures Peter Licavoli, Angelo Meli, Mike Rubino, William Tocco, and Carl Renda, among many lesser-known gangsters.

These hearings were the first live media event broadcast in the new television age when many Americans were buying their first television sets. Detroiters were amazed and outraged to learn the extent of mob influence in the United States economy. For the first time, viewers were able to see and hear testimony from some of the county's leading under-world gangsters. Longtime Detroiters wondered why there was hardly a mention of the Purple Gang in the Kefauver hearings. Not one former Purple Gang member was called to testify before the committee.

The reality was that the Purple Gang's long-term impact on organized crime was minimal. They went from petty criminals to big-time operators when they began supply-ing the Capone organization with Canadian whiskey, but after Prohibition was repealed, it was only a matter of time before the Purples were all washed up as an organization.

Acknowledgments

THIS BOOK WOULD NOT be possible without the assistance of several organizations and individuals. First, I would like to thank the docents of the Burton Historical Collection at the Detroit Public Library, the Windsor Public Library in Canada, the Detroit Historical Society, and the Walter Reuther Library of Labor and Urban Affairs for the use of their archives in the making of *The Elusive Purple Gang: Detroit's Kosher Nostra*.

Special thanks to Chris Edwards and Elaine Weeks of Walkerville Publishing for providing valuable background on Canada's role during United States Prohibition, and their guided tour of Walkerville, Ontario, ground zero for Detroit's illegal liquor trade of the 1920s and 1930s.

My heartfelt gratitude goes to genealogist Lois Kamoi for the use of her extensive Purple Gang family tree research which provided a touchstone that informs my entire book. Her insights into Jewish American culture were most helpful in telling the Purple Gang's early story. It was a pleasure working with her.

I neglected to recognize freelance San Diego copy editor Jean Jenkins for her help with my Amazon 2016 bestseller *Terror In Ypsilanti,* so I decided to use Jean's editing skills again and correct the oversight with this book project. Jean's willingness to work with me—an emerging author—and guide me along helped build my confidence to continue writing. Thank you, Jean.

Working with *Wheatmark Inc.* in Tucson, Arizona, is always a pleasure. Owner Sam Henrie, business manager Grael Norton, and project manager Lori Conser are the people behind my books. Their professionalism and care is reflected in the quality of their products. Congratulations on a decade of working together.

And finally, enough cannot be said for the Detroit press corps that reported on Prohibition Detroit at their personal peril. Journalists from the *Detroit Free Press*, the *Detroit Times*, and the *Detroit News* recorded events in real time which live on in the public record a century after they occurred. Many key public, government, and judicial documents are no longer available. Once again, the Fourth Estate proves its worth by documenting history for posterity. If for no other reason, the American press deserves our respect and gratitude.

Further Reading

Bergreen, Laurence. *Capone: The Man and the Era.* New York: Simon & Schuster, 1944.

Binder, John J. *Al Capone's Beer Wars.* Amherst, New York: Prometheus Books, 2017.

Buccellato, James A. *Early Organized Crime in Detroit: Vice, Corruption, and the Rise of the Mafia.* Charleston, SC: The History Press, 2015.

Buhk, Tobin T. *True Crime Michigan: The State's Most Notorious Criminal Cases.* Mechanicsburg, PA: Stackpole Books, 2011.

Burnstein, Scott M. T*he Detroit True Crime Chronicles: Tales of Murder and Mayhem in the Motor City.* Philadelphia: Camino Books Incorporated, 2013.

———. *Motor City Mafia: A Century of Organized Crime in Detroit.* Chicago: Arcadia Publishing, 2006.

Edwards, Chris, and Elaine Weeks. *The Best of Times Magazine: Stories from the Walkerville Times.* Windsor, ON: Walkerville Publishing, 2006.

Francis, Daniel. *Closing Time: Prohibition, Rum-Run-*

ners, and Border Wars. Madeira Park, BC: Douglas &
McIntyre, 2013.

Gervais, Marty. *The Rumrunners: A Prohibition Scrapbook*.
Windsor, ON: Biblioasis, 1980.

Gouth, George. *Booze, Boats & Bad Times: Recalling
Wyandotte's Dark Days of Prohibition*. Wyandotte, MI:
Wyandotte Historical Society, 2008.

Johnson, Stephen C. *Detroit Beer: A History of Brewing
in the Motor City*. Charleston, SC: The History Press,
2016.

Kavieff, Paul R. *The Purple Gang: Organized Crime in
Detroit (1910–1945)*. Fort Lee, NJ: Barricade Books,
2000.

————. *The Violent Years: Prohibition and the Detroit
Mobs*. Fort Lee, NJ: Barricade Books, 2001.

Knapp, Robert. *Small-Town Citizen Minion of the Mob:
Sam Garfield's Two Lives*. Clare, MI: Cliophile Press,
2018.

Kobler, John. *Capone: The Life and Legend of Al Capone*.
New York: Da Capo Press, 1971.

Mason, Philip P. *Rumrunners and the Roaring Twenties:
Prohibition on the Michigan-Ontario Waterway*.
Detroit: Great Lakes Books, 1995.

Okrent, Daniel. *Last Call: The Rise and Fall of Prohibition*.
New York: Scribner, 2010.

Pearson, Craig, and Daniel Wells. *The Windsor Star: From
the Vault* (Volume 1). Windsor, ON: Biblioasis, 2015.